WRISTON SPEAKING

WRISTON SPEAKING

A SELECTION OF ADDRESSES

BY

HENRY M. WRISTON
PRESIDENT OF BROWN UNIVERSITY
1937-1955

BROWN UNIVERSITY PRESS
PROVIDENCE, RHODE ISLAND
1957

Contents

vi

Preface

I N THE course of my tenure at Brown University there are on record something over a thousand speeches, not including those made spontaneously in such situations as a college president too often finds himself when he is unexpectedly called on for "a few words of inspiration."

From this mass of material a committee consisting of the Honorable Allyn L. Brown, Mr. W. Chesley Worthington, and Miss Ruth E. Sandborn has selected the addresses, reports, and articles here presented. Many of them have been severely cut. Moreover, it should be remembered that a large majority are speeches rather than essays, which have a quite different rhythm; in speaking much depends upon the tone of voice, the change of pace, the gesture, and other means of indicating emphasis, nearly all of which are lacking when the spoken word is reduced to print.

No attempt has been made to bring the selections up to date. The time of delivery is indicated in every instance, so that the period to which each belongs is readily identifiable. They were chosen as characteristic utterances rather than as a comprehensive coverage of the vast number of things about which a man in public or semi-public life is called upon to speak.

I want to express my gratitude to the Corporation of Brown University which directed the publication, to the committee which is responsible for the choices, and to

Miss Sandborn for editing and Mrs. Dorothea T. Borden for preparing the manuscript.

HENRY M. WRISTON

Providence, Rhode Island
March 16, 1957

PART I ✍ *A Point of View*

I ✍ The College Presidency
in Retrospect

I T IS probably immoral to encourage any man to enter his anecdotage even a moment earlier than necessary. Perhaps the management of this institute may be forgiven for having beaten the deadline by so little—or maybe they decided that I had unconsciously passed into that state—a not infrequent occurrence in our business.

What I have to say takes its text—i.e. a point of departure—from the remark of a friend who was a famous banker. He said: "Unless I guard against it every moment I find that I am not running the bank; the bank is running me." Certainly any college or university president very long in the business knows how easy it is to let the institution run him.

When I realized that it was happening to me, I sought to find out how and why. The first culprit was the mail. I would approach the office with my mind full of things I wanted to do. On the top of the pile of mail would be one of those letters with what might be called a standard opening: "Sir, you cur." This affected my blood pressure, drove every constructive thought from my head—and put

Institute for College and University Administrators, Harvard University, June 24, 1955

me instantly on the defensive. Why it always seemed necessary to try to prove the writer wrong I have never figured out. Certainly no correspondent in that era ever accepted my proof.

The next letter in the pile might ask a sensible question, but the reply would require a review of earlier correspondence—and maybe some vote of the governing boards—to be helpful and honest. That took time and further postponed getting at what had once been on my mind, but which was now fast fading.

You know what was in the rest of the pile: an invitation to give an inspirational address (fighting words with me) at the opening and dedication of a "new and enlarged" parking garage; a series of perfectly routine letters that anyone could answer—or to which no answer would be the most appropriate response.

Almost without fail the mail contained at least one questionnaire: the salaries of assistants in the several departments; the range of salaries of full professors with an explanation of the spread and of the intermediate amounts; to what did I attribute spring fever and the urge to break windows. Any questionnaire, even a good one (a contradiction in terms), would send my blood pressure up a few more notches and bad ones (a tautology) still further.

Before the pile was finished the appointments began—and my idea was at least sleeping, and probably dead. My first rule for running the college, instead of being run by it, came to be this: never look at the mail until it has been sorted, with the relevant previous material assembled and attached; all routine replies should be drafted by someone else; inquiries which other officers could answer as well or better ought to be referred to the appropriate person;

if courtesy required my signature, the replies could at least be drafted by the man—or woman—who was able to do it most effectively.

This solution provided some freedom from the tyrannous character of the mail. I could do what was in my mind to do when I came to the office—and do it while it was still fresh and could be done zestfully. At least, I was not taking dictation as to my activities from every Tom, Dick, and Harry in or out of the educational world, but, in any event, at a distance. I need not confuse my mind with a whole series of disparate (not to say inconsistent) decisions—or evasions—a chopped up mess of thought, disordered if not disorderly, because someone, somewhere, chose that instant, with the help or hindrance of Uncle Sam's mail, to raise a question which was on *his* mind—but not on mine.

No longer do I let someone else—usually with no responsibility in the matter, and not much concern even—tell me what to do. Is there any surer way to let the college or university run the president—and run him ragged—instead of having him run the institution than to look first at the mail?

Of course, I have known college presidents to take this prescription the way a college friend of mine took medicine. He was nervous before a track meet and had a touch of indigestion. He asked a drug clerk for something and was served a mixture of pepsin and soda. My friend asked anxiously if it was good for him; the clerk—with all his practical knowledge of psychosomatic medicine—said it certainly was. Whereupon my friend called for another dose.

Following this principle some college presidents not only put off reading the mail until later, they never read it at all. It is true that much mail, unread long enough, requires no answer. But the technique is bad for public relations. When everyone else has done what he can, there is an irreducible minimum which the president must answer—and the more promptly the better, so long as it does not deflect him from those things upon which his mind is alerted and his heart set.

The second insidious way in which the college can run the president—and to the damage of both—is by giving him no time to read or write. There are always more things to be done than any man can do. Reading can be put off; it does not seem so urgent or immediate as some other things. But the plain fact is that reading is a professional matter; it is an official duty. Therefore it is not marginal, not something to go to sleep on. If it does not have a very high priority, it does not get done. And the longer it does not get done, the lower its priority becomes. By and by reading is abandoned, though the pretense is preserved.

Meanwhile the making of speeches goes on—and on— and on. But a mind not refilled is soon emptied. Then the clichés take over. Every speech tends to rely upon a good story (all too often it is "the" good story), the gracious word, the technique of filling time, saying less and less.

Any speaker who pretends he does not repeat is fooling no one—unless he fools himself, the easiest mark after all. When you reach into the barrel, be sure to keep a record of your sin. It will save the embarrassment of repeating the same thing in the same place too often. And beware the extemporaneous—if you are driven to it, take a tape recording, and have it typed. Then read it and shudder—and sin no more!

The only suggestion I have to offer for securing the time essential for reading and writing is an extra office, where you can go and be "unavailable." It should have a separate secretary, a combination of bibliographer, editor, critic, and stenographer, who keeps a close record of what you have said, when and where, which speeches are new and which patchwork—I almost said crazy-quilt—made up of fragments of worn out verbal garments. And ideas become tatterdemalion more quickly than rayon.

I did not discover this; it was thrust upon me. One day, while a young man, I was called to the President's office. He told me to prepare a speech in order to substitute for him in a synthetic emergency. Then he said: "I was asked to make a speech during Education Week. There was no excuse or escape; I had to accept. But I have concentrated so much on raising money that I no longer have anything to say. You get ready and on the appointed day I will be 'ill' and send you as a substitute." Tragic; but at least he had found out about himself and did not carry on an empty pretense—as many another has done.

This argument is of no great significance if being a college president is a passing episode in a wide-ranging life. But for one who is going into administration as a profession, it is vital to keep an urgent appointment with yourself to read and to write. If you dictate speeches, revise and revise again. It is astonishing how verbiage can shrink through revision and how the cogency of an argument is enhanced when the prose is lean without adipose adjectives and adverbs to soften and conceal its bony structure, if any.

This is a hard gospel and the labor is fatiguing. I once complained to my father that after a speech I felt exhausted. His somewhat sardonic response was that I should praise God if my audience was not equally spent. Speaking, like reading, is nothing to be done on marginal time or with an economy of effort. There is no phase of administrative activity where careful preparation and thoughtful concentration pay higher dividends than in the inevitable and all too frequent speech making.

The third factor that tends to make the college run the president appears when he tries to do everything that a president ought to do. A college president is not only, as Marjorie Nicholson tersely expressed it, "the recipient of the ultimate buck"; he is responsible for an extremely wide range of activities—so wide, indeed, that if he tries to learn them all at once, much less do them all at once, he is certain to bog down. In fact, it takes several decades to learn his job in all its aspects. I shall retire with many lessons unlearned.

For example, it has been my misfortune to spend 30 years in the real estate business. Both institutions I have served are located in the heart of a community and in one of the better, if not the best, residential sections. The logic of institutional growth was far too obvious and the attempt to acquire necessary property sometimes seemed like submitting to a holdup. Learning how to cope with this problem is a full-time job in itself. It requires a deviousness which, if applied to other phases of their work, would justify the general reputation that is given to college presidents of being somewhat less than candid. Of course, many college presidents do not have to face any such real estate operations. Those in that happy circumstance should utter a prayer of thanksgiving, remembering, however, that they can easily become mired in some other phase of essential activity.

A related aspect of a college president's work which

must be learned is architecture. In this field the president must not only be an expert in aesthetics (that is the simplest phase); he must be responsible for the design of buildings which please the modernist and also the traditionalist; but he must never compromise between the two, for that is unsatisfactory to both. In Brown we have an unusual government—two boards meet simultaneously in the same room with two presiding officers and one secretary with concurring action by both boards required to pass any motion. In over 18 years the only time the Fellows and the Trustees divided about any issue was on the question of the use of modern or Georgian architecture; the Fellows, the senior body whose average age is at least ten years higher than that of the Trustees, voted for modern; the Trustees voted for Georgian. This illustrates the simplicity of the problem of pleasing everyone.

Even more difficult is the care one must take in the design of buildings. An architect can seldom give you something good you do not know you want. He is almost certain to give you something you do not want unless you have a very precise knowledge of what you desire. What you want is not to be determined by inspiration but by hard study and analysis. Only so can you bring your requirements within reach of your financing while sacrificing nothing in the functioning of the building. Thin partitions in a dormitory will save money on construction, but you will pay for them many times over in noise and consequent disciplinary problems. The perfect classroom has yet to be designed, but unless it is designed within your administration you will be held accountable.

There may be a college president somewhere who does not need any buildings. If so, he is in a position to pray the prayer of the Pharisee, thanking God "that I am not as other men." But if he exalteth himself in this matter, he will be abased in some other. Even if he does not have to buy land or build buildings, he must still raise money. This is not only the most exhausting and frustrating of all his activities, it is a technical problem of the first order of difficulty.

How much butter should be used in dealing with people with funds? How far should one go in making commitments as to the use to which money will be put? What limitations are of no serious import and which are fatal? How much should the president do himself and how much can he do by deputy? There is the famous instance of the Mount Holyoke drive when a certain manufacturer of a needless product, widely used especially on the under side of theater seats, was asked for money. He coldly replied that he was accustomed to have the begging done by presidents and not by deputies. I have known an instance where college policy was deflected for a matter of 20 years to please a man who died intestate, having strung officials along for two decades.

Even these difficulties in raising money are far from being the most serious problem; the strain on character is the most taxing. Do you describe to the prospect what is presently there or are you moved by your own visions into setting them forth as current reality? Have your hopes and ambitions run ahead of the actual situation so far that the two are out of touch? I recall a famous protest by the senior member of a faculty who said in a rather quavering tone, "Ooooh, it is not proper to say that the President is a liar. It is undeniable that what he says bears no relationship to the facts, but to be a liar one must consciously deviate from the truth, and he has been saying those things so long that he actually believes them." Let me add that the President was an extremely successful money raiser and had built up the student body; his resignation was requested on other grounds; he was not a scholar and intellectual leader.

A president must not only buy land and build buildings and beg incessantly, he must be continuously strengthening the faculty. In a college the president has a direct, immediate, and very lively participation in this matter, particularly when the numbers are small enough so that there is not a strong departmental organization. But even where the recommendation of a chairman is the basis upon which nominations are accepted or rejected, the final responsibility rests with the president.

In reaching a decision, how much attention should he pay to character, to personality, and to scholarship in a prospective teacher? There are sharp differences of opinion about all these matters. I remember a number of recommendations made to me which guaranteed the nonappointment of the recommended persons. They ran this way: "The man will never be good enough to teach in a university, but he will do well in a small college." This was a revelation of the feebleness of the man's scholarship. It is of a piece with the many suggestions that for college teaching there should be a cheap degree which does not require a man to do research, lest he know something that he need not use. Scholarship is a primary essential.

As for character, one should do his best to look to integrity, but should not confuse religious irregularity or personal habits (like smoking 30 years ago) with character. As for personality, one must look to the long pull and not to the short. I have known the glib and the genial, the apple-polisher and the careerist to make a strong first impression at the time of the appointment, which turned terribly sour three years later. And the man whose silence and apparent impassivity scared me most turned out to be one of the greatest young teachers I ever knew. When you are forming a responsible judgment, either on your own initiative or in dealing with the recommendation from a department, you are on slippery ground. If you do not make mistakes, you are a genius. It will be a real test of your own character whether you are ready to face the consequences involved in correcting your mistakes.

The precepts used in deciding what candidates to take, the conservatism or liberality or rashness with which promises are made are all matters of greatest difficulty. Looking back on my own experience, I now know that the place where I told the most lies was during the early years in explaining to professors whom I wanted to appoint what I hoped to do for them. Because of an ancient hallucination that presidents are omnipotent many of them believed I could and would do as I hoped to do. Taking my visions for promises, they accepted the appointment, not only to be disillusioned by what they experienced; they were also disheartened as to my character.

Bitter experience led to a practice which has since avoided many misunderstandings. No matter how simple the conference, make a record of it. It is best to dictate a summary in the presence of the man to whom you have been talking and give him a free hand to make corrections. In any event, the record should be made promptly. If the professor has not heard it dictated, send him two copies, asking for the return of one either corrected or initialed. Whenever I have failed to observe this routine with religious fidelity, the results have been unhappy.

It is not so hard to keep a strong department strong, for people in an outstanding department are not afraid of new competition. Building up a weak department requires insights of the most extraordinary kind. Members of such departments will not present the strongest candidates, and there will be a great temptation on their part to frustrate strong, independent appointments.

Even when one has surmounted all these obstacles, the care and feeding of professors is an art in itself. I do not need to point out that salaries, whatever they are, are *ipso facto* miserable; they always have been and will always be wretched. Our first obligation is to make them less wretched. Only when that is done with vigor and sincerity can one begin to stress the moral and spiritual compensations which go with teaching. I make what may be interpreted as a cynical remark: the moral and spiritual compensations are almost in inverse ratio to the wretchedness of the monetary compensation.

But there are other things which can be done; there are what might be called "fringe benefits." A policy of active generosity in the matter of sabbaticals and leaves of absence pays heavy dividends. It is worth accepting great inconveniences to let professors go elsewhere for a time to gain new experiences and broaden their contacts.

Another potent aid to faculty satisfaction is what I define as obedience to the eleventh commandment: thou shalt not commit. As a young member of the faculty I served on committees that did administrative work, that did manual labor, such as hanging the Japanese lanterns at commencement. I did more irrelevant things than were necessary and in such small matters as lack of telephone service and occasional stenographic help was forced to waste time and effort. These "savings" looked all right in the public budget, but were costly in the invisible budget that is much more important than the optical illusion which is usually presented to trustees as "the budget."

If a professor teaches and studies and sees students, that is about all one should ever ask of him. Administrative officers are the servants of the faculty and they ought to serve and not to govern, and certainly ought never to rule. I know colleges where faculty people are tied up two or three days a week with committee work from 4 o'clock on. The administrative costs look low in the budget; however, instructional time and study time are wasted on inefficient administration. Moreover, there is a steady warping of perspective as a consequence of eternally hashing over the trivia that come before most committees. If these services were taken into account under administrative costs where they belong, the expense of instruction would shrink and that of administration would burgeon.

Parenthetically, if a president does not learn to be a fairly competent accountant, he soon loses control of his institution either to the business officers or to the auditors. These are two potential enemies; one of them can become a strong ally; auditors, however, tend to remain perpetually in an adverse relationship; they are not very sympathetic to educational problems and seldom read the charters which set forth the powers of governing boards. The chances of making an ally of the business officer are in direct proportion to the president's mastery of accounting problems and procedures and a very realistic appreciation of how sketchy college cost accounting is.

The profit and tax incentives which have led to the elaboration of cost accounting in business are absent in the college; furthermore the historical record of plant account, the absence of depreciation, the failure to allocate charges, and a thousand other details—some of them minuscle and some of them of large import—make college accounting a separate business by itself. I remember with bitterness being asked at the end of my first year to say how much deficit should be shown. I had innocently believed that the deficit was the deficiency of income beneath outgo. When I found that in order to conceal the actual amount they had charged library books to capital, which meant paying for them out of endowment, I decided the moment had come to learn not merely the rudiments but the intricacies of the budget and accounting.

That is the end of the parenthesis. I return to the care and feeding of professors, which are closely related to this matter because promotions are too often governed by the budget. Sometimes the president plays by ear, sometimes advances are made automatically and let the devil take the hindmost on the budget. This raises the fundamental question whether there should be a formula such as was previously used (and still may be) in the Faculty of Arts and Sciences in Harvard, whereby appointments were dependent upon vacancies, or whether promotions should be made on the basis of individual merit without reference to any formula.

I have found it useful to maintain what I call a pattern of the faculty members. It is a confidential book, with carefully cross-indexed pages, showing their ages, length of service, length of service in each grade, the relationship which all those things bear to salary, and a number of other things. It seems to me that departmentalism can be carried too far in building a faculty; it is more important not to have too many professors retiring at once, not to have either too much stability or too much turnover (both matters of judgment and not of formula) than to have any fixed plan of promotion. The beds upon which the faculty lie are hard enough without making them Procrustean.

Perhaps institutions of great age and size and relatively great wealth can assume more rigid attitudes in this matter than those who have to exhibit an immediate and personal concern for individual faculty members, if they are to work harmoniously as a team.

There is only one other point of view that I need to express: I believe the simpler the relationship between the president and the faculty the better. One of my friends, upon his appointment at Brown, talked to me about University housing. I said (he considered rather cruelly) that anyone who could not find a place to live was not very resourceful. After ten years he thinks my opinion was correct. If the institution is landlord it either gives more service than other landlords (and is under criticism from those who are not tenants) or it does not (and is under criticism from those who are tenants). It makes for a further complication of relationships. We already have TIAA, CREF, Social Security, group insurance, Blue Cross, Blue Shield, and how many other things I do not know. As these services multiply, they make more sensitive points than are desirable. Of course, relationships cannot be confined to salary—and nothing else. But unduly to multiply them is to create problems and is, I think, a mistake.

Some of you may be not only intellectually but physically restless because I have mentioned so many aspects of the president's labors which he must learn—but cannot master all at once—without ever referring thus far to his educational leadership, a phrase I am tempted to put in quotation marks.

One faculty member in a well-known and distinguished institution said that the president's educational leadership consisted in going to meetings, listening with half his mind to what was said, and then coming home and imitating projects he did not fully understand. It was a savage comment, but contained more than a grain of truth. The plain fact is that with all his other preoccupations the president will have to read and study, reflect and cogitate more than most do in order to exercise imaginative leadership over any considerable period of time. In general he must be hospitable and sensitive to suggestions and not too deeply concerned with their originality. The dangers lie in getting administrative affairs so over-organized that they lose their freshness, that teaching loses its zest, that routine takes the place of excitement and drive.

If a president remains long enough in the business, it becomes clear that there are cyclical movements in reform. One must avoid cynicism, therefore, when something is proposed anew which was practiced 30 years before. Every reform carries the seeds of its own decay; there is nothing wrong, consequently, with a return to an old approach if it is done with new knowledge, fresh insights, and zestful energy. Let us take one or two examples, such as admission with advanced standing. That was quite common when I went to college; indeed, I entered with advanced standing on examination upon work I did in high school. Consider graduation in less than four years. There was a time when, I think, nearly a third of the students at Harvard did that. While I did not quite do that, I did finish the work for both the bachelor's and the master's degrees in four years. That was not uncommon at that time, but abuses sprang up and the procedure was later abolished. Now reform has come full turn and with Foundation aid and a good deal of committee apparatus we are back, trying both experiments again.

A second observation is that the local situation needs

careful study and enormous patience. The most distinctive teaching reform we have had at Brown in my time was under contemplation in one form or another for nearly 15 years before circumstances were sufficiently propitious for it to become operative.

In education, as in politics, leadership is to some extent real and to some extent an optical illusion. The ideas are likely to come from elsewhere; it is the responsibility of the president to dramatize them and to expound them, negotiate their passage and facilitate their trial. If these functions are well performed, the results are often better than those which follow an attempt on his part to be the originator, the creator, and the actual leader.

The relationship of the president with the students is one of the most difficult of all his tasks. If he begins young enough, he may be mistaken for an undergraduate. As long as he is, he can be "one of the boys." In fact, when there is a considerable gap between the age of his predecessor and his own, even a mature man may carry with him certain illusions of youth for a time; it will be remarked with approval that he appeared in the locker room and took a vital interest in athletics. He had not yet been reduced to golf, but was able to play tennis and to throw a ball and play on the faculty baseball team without making a perfect ass of himself.

But the man who keeps that up a moment too long does not make himself popular; he just makes himself ridiculous. There comes a time when respect has to take the place of good fellowship, when "sir" becomes part of every sentence addressed to him. Then, if students refer to him by his first name or nickname, it may not be with affection but as a form of ridicule. Of course, the relationship varies sharply with a man's temperament and, I may say, even more sharply with the kind of deans he has: the better the deans, the less opportunity the president has to deal directly with young people.

I forbear to say much about the president's public relations. In the modern world they are extremely important, but pressure is often exerted to have him base public relations upon an entirely erroneous principle—namely to say only the things to which everyone will agree immediately, to put himself in a descending spiral of timidity, finally to say nothing at great length. I believe it is the responsibility of a president to have opinions and to express them with vigor and forthrightness and yet with as much tact as he can summon without losing the point. Particularly in dealing with the alumni it is essential to talk about educational matters and to treat them as adults and not pander to the group who think of nothing but athletics; they are a very small group who get far too much attention. But public relations are a side of the business that has to be learned.

Finally there is the relationship to the governing body, by whatever title or in whatever form. This must be one of complete candor; members should be kept informed, and interested if possible. Proposals ought to be advanced with a view to obtaining a consensus; they should be reshaped and modified until a consensus is in sight, or abandoned if compromise has ruined their substance. It is a mistake to press trustees too hard; a president should stop before the breaking point, remembering that some trustees are quite brittle.

May I recall to your mind—what time may well have eroded—that I am giving a brief list of things a president must learn. I began with the remark that he cannot do them all at once, lest he leap from duty to duty, performing none with any skill. This determines, so far as I am concerned, one's administrative philosophy. The president must do all these things, but he cannot do them all at once. Therefore, while he must do some of them all the time, he must do the others only from time to time; and he must find space in his calendar and energy when he does them at all to do them well—thoughtfully and completely.

Besides their sheer bulk, there is another reason why it is essential to attack some of them from time to time instead of all the time: it is to escape boredom. No president long in office will have difficulty in understanding what I mean. In a speech given at the inauguration of Miss McBride as President of Bryn Mawr, President Ada Comstock of Radcliffe told of President Charles William Eliot's remark that, while his life had been more varied and interesting than that of most men, "nineteen-twentieths of his work was drudgery, 'uninteresting repetitions of familiar strenuous exertions.'" I have known many presidents, not all of them so distinguished as Eliot, who told me their worst enemy in office was boredom. Boredom can be escaped by varying the emphasis in one's duties. I have found that the greatest single source of refreshment is to change the zone of my own activities from time to time.

In order to do this it is clear that one has to deputize some of the duties, but none of them in perpetuity. This has a marked effect upon one's administrative theory and practice. If one is devoted to rigid design and likes a chart of the organization of the university or college bureaucracy that he can paste on his wall, he will make assignments which can be changed only by involving a rebuke to the person relieved of his duties. Long ago, therefore, I adopted a fluid type of administration. There is no clear definition of what a dean should do or what a business officer should do or what a registrar should do; the authority or the influence exercised by those people depends, as do the influence and authority of the president, upon the personality and the adaptability of those who from time to time hold the office.

Often they, too, get bored with the "uninteresting repetitions of familiar strenuous exertions." One must, therefore, watch his administrative colleagues and, at the first sign that they are bored or stale or fatigued, make such adjustments as bring to them the same refreshment that the president can find by varying the accent on his own activities.

For my part, I think there is another practical reason for a fluid administration: there are not so many boundary disputes. Two things can happen when a firm and formal assignment of deputized duties is made: a man will either stay away from the boundaries of his neighbor or he will crowd them. The first produces a vacuum and the second friction. If there is a zone of mutual activity, they tend to work together better and there are not so many appeals to the president to settle quarrels. If there are occasional conferences in his office as to which one shall take over a project, the assignment ceases to be a matter of *amour-propre* and becomes one of convenience.

All this may be taken as a horrible confession by some of my colleagues in the craft. However, if I had it to do over again, I would turn to this theory of administration earlier, and apply it more freely.

I think it tragic that the tenure of many presidents is so short, that so many run afoul of trustees who are men of good will but without *expertise* in a field which is highly complicated and very technical, where the analogies to business are often more deceptive than revealing and where business ideas, when transferred, become the enemies of good college administration. We have in America a unique governing relationship; the varieties of charters, the multiplication of bylaws, and the differences in size, objectives, and resources make each institution a separate problem. There is room in higher education, however, for the professional administrator—the person who gives his whole working life to it. In this career he can find profound satisfactions, his own share of good, clean fun, and a rich deep-down joy—as well as some frustration, many disappointments, and occasional heartbreak.

II ☞ Liberal Arts at Mid-Century

THE liberal arts, of course, have a long history. In modern times, however, they are taught in two quite different types of institutions—liberal arts colleges and universities. In his recent report to the alumni, President A. Whitney Griswold of Yale began by saying, "If we were looking for a title for the history of American institutions of higher education an appropriate one would be 'How the Liberal Arts College Became a University.' " He then proceeded to point out that historically the universities had become so engrossed in so many problems that there had been a strong tendency for them to swallow up the liberal arts. He wondered whether as appropriate a title for the next 50 years might prove to be "How the University Strengthened Its Liberal Arts College," repaying, thus, an ancient debt.

Perhaps the situation has never been defined so explicitly in such brief terms. There can be no doubt whatever that the idea of the modern university, in the American sense, is not much over 75 years old; a century would cover it surely, though there had been earlier previsions of what might ultimately happen. Certainly, too, in many universities the liberal arts have now been pretty effec-

University of Alabama Faculty, March 11, 1955

tively swallowed up. Indeed, the college of arts, letters, and science in some of the great public institutions is often a kind of service agency for the rest of the university and is not in fact, as it is regarded in theory, the heart and center of its program.

If one were to set a date when this trend toward the engulfment of the arts was established, he might select the turn of the century. It was then that the elder Robert La Follette as governor of Wisconsin promoted the "Wisconsin idea," a phrase which became a kind of trade mark. His central thought was that it was not task enough for the university to train youth; in addition, it had the obligation to perform direct services to the state which gave it support. The program of the university was to be developed in such a manner that no urgent demand of the state should go unanswered by the university.

The Wisconsin idea, although widely discussed at the time, did not pervade the university world until the first World War. Aside from the agricultural colleges, there was relatively little tendency for educational institutions to be utilized for purposes of commerce or industry or government or national defense. Institutions of higher education pursued their own way of life; they were as separate from government and business as were the churches. Indeed, the life of the mind was far closer to the life of the spirit than to "practical affairs."

In my youth the adequacy of the liberal arts went unchallenged, even when universities took on other responsibilities (like "agriculture and the mechanic arts" as the Morrill Act so quaintly called them). In fact the Morrill Act itself explicitly protected the position of "scientific and classical studies." In those days I never heard colleges criticized for their distinctive position in our society; no one expected them to perform otherwise than they did. The teacher, like the preacher, was judged by standards different from those applicable to the business man.

The first World War brought great changes. It led to emergency employment of previously unexploited utilitarian capacities. Professors were drawn into new governmental administrative agencies; research projects on poison gas and like activities were launched; military training to supply officers in haste absorbed many institutions; industry, cut off from German dyes and other essentials, set up research departments staffed in part by professors. When one looks back upon those activities, there comes a keen remembrance of how temporary they were supposed to be. But a thin edge of the wedge had been inserted and the ultimate effect proved to be profound.

At the close of the war there ensued a rash of endowment campaigns. The tone of the appeals marked a turning point in the history of American higher education. They were keyed to a more adequate salary scale for professors; the new argument was that these men were deserving not alone because of their traditional services in educating youth and in seeking truth; they deserved better salaries, also, because of their practical skills in morale building, in the economics of the war, and their useful research both for weapons and for industry. It was now for the first time suggested that the colleges must compete with industry for men learned in science, economics, and other fields. The professor was suddenly valued on a new scale which had nothing to do with the liberal arts. The new estimate was superimposed upon the old one and tended to obscure it. Money poured in during the twenties in unprecedented amounts.

What had been uniquely the Wisconsin idea now became generalized; it expanded far beyond any expectations of Governor La Follette. So true is this that few people now remember the phrase, once so well known. It is hardly an exaggeration to say that the idea was carried so far after the war that some institutions came to be regarded as a kind of one-stop service station which would perform a myriad of tasks in the public interest. Faculty members whose learned skills had an active market in industry and those who could serve the state directly came to have higher salaries than those who taught the liberal studies whose basic aim was the preparation of youth to use and enjoy—and protect—liberty.

Students who entered college after the first World War began to bring a new kind of motivation to college. I cannot remember a classmate of mine who came to college to gain a vocational advantage. After the war many, if not most, had that idea uppermost in their minds. Indeed, many tended to be suspicious of the liberal arts; the ivory tower had come into disrepute. There was an insistent demand for practical skills; young people resisted the classical disciplines; they even preferred technology to science; they wanted business in place of economics. By and large the universities obliged, and curricula were not only enormously expanded, but the balance was tipped toward immediately marketable skills.

What one war began, the next accelerated and expanded beyond belief. Only in the universities were scientists available for atomic research; the first chain reaction was achieved in a university. That was symbolic: institutions were drawn into the main stream of defense, of administration, of training. The whole rhythm of their lives was altered.

Though the war was over nearly a decade ago, universities have not yet recovered their own way of life. So vast, so diverse, so intimately tied with business and government are programs of both teaching and research that there is danger that the function of teaching the liberal arts will become an adjunct, while what should be the universities' incidental service becomes the principal occupation. Institutional costs have increased so rapidly, new resources have accumulated so relatively slowly, that "earned income" from research and direct services has mounted to well over half the total institutional income in some conspicuous instances. Today no physics department in any great university could carry forward its current program without government money; something like the same statement could be made about several other university departments.

I was trained as a historian; therefore I know that the historical process is irreversible. In what I have been recounting there is no trace of nostalgia for "the good old days." I would not wish the colleges and universities to return to the status of 1914. If I am tempted, sometimes, to feel that today they are being carried along in swift currents away from the liberal arts, I am sure they were then in a backwater—and one that was always in danger of becoming stagnant. Better the dangers associated with vital relationships with public affairs than the decay inherent in worship of tradition.

Moreover, the introduction of many subjects quite irrelevant to the main task helped break down barriers that had excluded things of infinite value. The ancient college considered itself the chief exponent of the liberal arts; yet it omitted one of the principal elements of the quadrivium —music. Not even its history was noted; enjoyment of its great works had no part in the program of the college; participation in making music was confined largely to glee and mandolin clubs—extracurricular singing of second-rate songs and playing trivial music, at about the level of singing commercials.

There may still be places so obscurantist in spirit as to argue whether singing or playing an instrument is sufficiently "intellectual" to be properly part of a curriculum, but none is so backward that it would exclude the history of music, the principles of harmony, and appreciation. Students today hear more good music and make more good music than ever before. When given the choice of what to sing, they almost uniformly choose the best.

The curriculum of the pre-World War traditional college not only by-passed music; it knew nothing whatever of art. In this respect, also, reform has been swift and sweeping. One of the great universities is still inquiring whether drawing, painting, sculpture are adequately intellectual to justify "credit," but in most institutions an affirmative decision has long been made. "Intellectual" can no longer be so narrowly defined as to exclude all creative effort except the verbal. The history of art, the analysis and appreciation of art (including architecture) are firmly embedded in the modern curriculum. Students see more pictures, see better pictures, and make better pictures than ever before.

Drama, like music and art, has come into its own. In many traditional colleges no one thought a student play important. The number of college theaters early in the century was insignificant. Today nearly every institution has a reasonably well-equipped theater, and college productions often have finish and style. A student who enlarges his understanding of a play by acting in it is no longer considered a mere mummer or mime, or puppet; to learn meaning by entering into the action is at last legitimate. Teachers no longer concentrate wholly on the origin of plot, the techniques, the linguistics, the influence of others upon the author—on everything, in short, save the writing itself.

Culture is less on the defensive than ever before in this generation. Listening rooms in libraries and dormitories are thronged with students who want to hear recordings made by poets, actors, musicians. They live among better pictures—they are more alert to quality—than ever before. The humanities are emerging into a better perspective and, without discounting scholarship, are once more stressing writing as a work of art.

Amidst current lamentations over the decline of the liberal arts we should take heart because the program has been greatly enriched. We have broken away from Puritan inhibitions; the aesthetic values of music and art and drama and poetry are recognized to a degree quite novel in American history.

Moreover, competition from newer subjects has been a boon to teaching in the older disciplines. Monopoly has the same debilitating effect upon instruction as upon enterprise. Competition is the life of teaching as of trade. The monopoly long enjoyed by mathematics, the classics, and foreign languages has been broken. Into some places that had become stodgy have come energy, originality, zest.

I do not mean to say that everything is perfect "in this best of all possible worlds." There is need for more than the changes in substance which have been so heartening. There must be further changes in method and in curricular structure if the liberal arts are to exercise the vital influence which their tradition and their values justify.

It may be argued that in disciplines as old as the liberal arts there is not much opportunity for new ideas which can be applied to teaching. Nonetheless, those who have responsibility for administration must send up a veritable fountain of ideas. Not all the ideas will be new, but the fountain should contain some new ones to take the place of those that evaporate in the air or spill over into the gutter.

Let us be candid: if our educational progress were wholly dependent upon new ideas, the situation would be hopeless. The fountain, therefore, should be like some of the most beautiful I have ever seen, recirculating what has many times been cast up and fallen back. Thus, even if the ideas in the fountain are, for the most part, the same ideas, constant flowing will keep them aerated so that they do not become stagnant.

We should not mourn ideas lost through evaporation before acceptance; for the most part such thoughts had too low an order of stability; they were like some of those evanescent chemical elements which are never found in a pure state, and, when isolated, disappear with startling rapidity. But when an idea proves stable in structure and has been accepted by the academic community, the administrative officers must see that it is not then destroyed by evaporation. Yet this is an all too common occurrence.

I have known instances where a well-conceived graduation requirement was destroyed, not by action of the faculty nor by action of a governing board, but by a series of almost unnoticed "interpretations" by a registrar. The end product was a practice which had no logic, no coherence. In short, the idea behind the original legislation had evaporated, leaving only a bureaucratic practice.

I recall a piece of timber taken from the Brown University library; its surface was intact, but termites had eaten the substance away until only a paper-thin shell was left. Such a situation is rare with termite-infested wood; it is common enough in academic administration. Officers have a profound responsibility to see that instruction is not eroded. This requires the most extraordinary perception and the employment of methods similar to those of an intelligence agency. I ought not to have to say that intelligence work does not consist in spying, though governments do employ spies. We all know that most intelligence work needs no such secret aid; it consists in the alert and perceptive observation of data which pass for the most part unnoticed but are available to anyone who takes the trouble to look.

Good intelligence work about teaching, for example, involves listening to the overtones and the undertones of what students say in the course of normal conferences about their instruction. What the student says in response to direct questioning must be heavily discounted; the number of distortions of all sorts, under such circumstances, is ordinarily so large as to vitiate the information. What he says when he does not know he is saying it—what flows from his stream of consciousness—is of greatest value. Of course, such data require interpretation in the light of what is known about the student. Of course, too, they must be compared and correlated with what other students have revealed. But by acuity of hearing, which takes account of frequency vibrations not usually noticed, the most valuable information about teaching is acquired.

A fair and useful evaluation of this information regarding the quality and standards of teaching is made by accretion, not by inspiration. A competent administrative officer can accumulate many scraps of information from many sources over a considerable period of time, and by correlating and synthesizing them skillfully he can form a responsible judgment.

The effective use of such information may easily be regarded as a threat to academic freedom. It is one of the tragedies of our situation that academic freedom seldom protects only the able, the conscientious, the inspired; too often it shields the incompetent and, far more often, the inept. To deal with a teacher who has a passion for lecturing but no skill at it, or one who thinks he can conduct a lively discussion, but talks all the time himself (he is a discussant and not a discussee), to meet these and many other situations requires a subtlety and a suppleness of approach which are difficult to achieve without falling into deviousness and cognate sins of which administrative officers are almost automatically adjudged guilty.

Nevertheless, the problem must be dealt with if the growth of the student is our objective, if he is the one whose interests we are obligated to serve. It must be faced by resolute and courageous, if tactful and courteous, means—and it may not safely be shirked. Colleges have been made intellectually bankrupt by tactical retreats, by timidity in personnel management, by using "public relations" as an alibi, by every sort of evasion to escape a plain duty because it is difficult.

Another arduous duty, from which there is no escape, lies within the province of liberal arts officers. They must fight, in season and out of season, and never yield though they die in the attempt, all endeavors to "save money" in instruction. I have seen it argued, indeed I have seen it "proved," that students can "learn" more science by demonstration lectures than by attendance upon laboratories. That particular "experiment" was a typical instance of economic determinism. The object of the "experiment" was to prove what the officers of the institution felt its finances required to be proved. There is no question that by shaping a certain kind of examination you can show that a student learns more by a given method than by some other. This is particularly true if the "other" instruction is in over-crowded laboratories, supervised by graduate students with no instructional interest, who go through the motions in order to get money for survival.

By adapting the examination you can prove that students "learn" more in a lecture than they do in a discussion. You can prove that students will "learn" more if a series of specialists deliver lectures that the students are expected to correlate by a process in which you do not trust the faculty member to succeed. When you begin with the premise that the students must learn what no faculty man is competent to teach, you start with an assumption which begs the question.

If colleges are not interested in stuffing the students in order to measure on an examination paper their retention of the stuffing, if they are trying to draw out the students and stimulate their growth, all "economy" devices are bound to be revealed for what they are—an effort to short-change the students for economic, rather than educational, reasons.

In too many American colleges too many courses consist of a series of lectures, with readings in a textbook, and an occasional test. It is inherently absurd to suppose that a student will learn best from a man he does not know and who does not know him, from a lecturer whose voice he hears, whose not too attractive facial characteristics are dimly familiar, and whose name he does not learn until the middle of the semester.

Common sense, backed by *all* experience, makes it evident that the student will develop more rapidly and more fully with someone whom he meets face to face, who tests his mind, and with whom he has some intelligent familiarity. Yet faculties have been known to condone measures which deprive the student of educational experience in order to give fiscal satisfaction to presidents, business officers, and governing boards.

Among my catalogue of obligations one of the principal ones is to stand at Armageddon and fight continuously, bitterly, and skillfully to keep the students in contact with books, and preferably with good books. An astonishing statistic in the average American college is the relatively small number of different books withdrawn from the library. An alarming percentage of that small number are secondary or mere textbooks. Sometimes the library figures seem much larger than I have indicated. This is easily accomplished; circulation can appear heavy if, in a class of reasonable size, enough duplicates are acquired and pages are assigned once or twice a week. In this meretricious fashion a very small number of books attain a very large statistical circulation with an infinitesimal intellectual result.

By reason of certain historical episodes which have marked the last 20 years (to which I make only an oblique reference), one is almost afraid to speak of great books. In using such a phrase one may be thought either to be accepting as final the list which was revealed to a bright young man near the shores of Lake Michigan or, even worse, one may seem to be trespassing upon his copyright. Both risks I must run, for the fact remains that the better the book the better the teaching and the better the learning.

Faculty members who find ways to insinuate good books into the hands of good students have performed a service beyond price. Many an undergraduate reaches his junior year and several their senior year and a few graduate without having touched a single book of the first order of excellence or significance in the intellectual development of mankind. The International Business Machines Corporation has a sign on every desk and on nearly every wall, "Think." It would be well if every teacher had a sign on his desk, and perhaps tattooed on his brow, "Books, books, books."

A correlative obligation is to harp insistently and persistently upon another string—that is to have the students write and, even more difficult, to have what they write read and, bordering upon the impossible, have it read by people who take a responsible relationship to its grammar, unity, coherence, and substance.

I was once involved in an experiment which showed concretely that English was the function of a department, not the college. It was agreed that the Chemistry department would turn its papers over to the English department. Incidentally one collateral result was that the Chemistry department thereby virtually confessed that it did not know how to judge the quality of the English in the papers. The experiment broke down almost immediately because one boy was given two grades upon his chemistry paper: an A by the Chemistry professor and an F by the English professor. Inasmuch as the "credit" was for Chemistry, the lad did not care what the English professor thought. Inasmuch as the English professor found his activities futile, he did not pursue them further.

There is overwhelming evidence that, unless all departments in an institution care about the quality of writing, the improvement essential to a real liberal education will not be made. Unless substantial essays are demanded in every course, unless they are read critically and returned with criticism and comment, we shall not make headway against the alarming "higher illiteracy" of our times. Every teacher must be the champion of writing. As he recites his litany about "Books, books, books," he can add another line, "Write, write, write."

This discussion draws me reluctantly to the next function of a faculty member. He must avoid confusion between meeting the requirements for a degree and acquiring an education. The root meaning of curriculum is a race course; moreover it is an "obstacle race." Presumably the course is not designed merely as a series of obstacles to make it difficult to get a degree; it is designed to make it more likely that the student who completes the course will also get an education. It is calculated to make the student test his various powers; its purpose is to see that he does not take an easy way around the barriers, that he does not avoid the effort and the discipline which a true education requires.

Nonetheless we must face the fact that the obstacle race is not perfectly constructed. This is partly because we do not know enough about human individuals to be able to make one design which will force every student into the exercise of his powers. It is also deficient because the average curriculum is so full of compromises among departmental and other special interests within the faculty that it is not so good as it ought to be. Indeed, it is not nearly so good as we know how to make it if we would lay aside our jealousies, prejudices, special interests, and personal idiosyncrasies.

Of course, the key weakness of a curriculum is that it has to serve as a guide for too many people whose talents, interests, capabilities, and energies vary so widely. The conclusion is inescapable that numerous students can meet every requirement for a degree and still avoid an education. They can do it by shrewd selection of courses. In this context the intelligence services open to them as to how to perform that feat far exceed the information available to the faculty, to say nothing of their ability to alter the situation. The student can get a degree by use of rote memory and avoidance of efforts at original thought. He can evade the courses that require essays and theses and find enough courses that give objective tests so that he never has to learn how to write. He can weave his devious way around the hurdles, over the low ones, under the high ones, and meet the statistical requirements without much intellectual gain.

This capacity to attain a degree while escaping an education accounts for the well-known fact that many alumni never pick up a book, naturally, for recreation. This explains why so many graduates display obscurantist views about economics, politics, security, international affairs, and many other topics that ought to challenge and engage their interest.

The faculty, therefore, must bring to bear all the resources at their command. Among these are reason, exposition, parental influence, fraternity and social pressure, competition, pride, whatever they can mobilize; a list of all the weapons in their armory would be formidable. With them the teacher can see that the student not only meets the requirements but also performs in such a way that he enjoys going over the obstacle course as an athlete over the hurdles, the high jump, the pole vault, or as a good football player enjoys the block, the tackle, and carrying the ball. The faculty will make sure that the student performs, in other words, in so zestful a manner that he gains an education and is never afraid that he will do better than he needs to do or that he will learn something not strictly required.

An academic officer has a special and difficult responsibility—to protect the integrity of the liberal arts. He must seek to make the concept really meaningful, first to the faculty, then to students. The plain fact is that liberal studies are subject to the operation of Gresham's law: bad coin tends constantly to drive out the good. I know a place where there is no department of economics in the college of liberal arts; all the instruction in that field is borrowed from the school of business administration. This is economical; it is efficient. But no elaborate demonstration is needed to point out that economics so taught will not be a liberal discipline; it will partake of the professional emphasis of the school from which it is drawn.

Many institutions without schools of business have rationalized the introduction of business courses into their economics departments. Being so located they are labeled as courses in liberal culture, whereas their whole tone and temper are different. This is no slander upon business administration; it has its own value and virtue. But the subject is not one properly to be classified among the liberal arts.

English composition and English literature have too often been taught by what can only be called an anti-liberal method. Courses in journalism, courses in drama with a professional or semi-professional purpose often masquerade as liberal studies. And some courses in literature are so tainted with the dregs of German *Wissenschaft* as to be utterly sterile in a liberal curriculum.

Many a beginning science course is taught, not with any concept of liberal learning, but as an introduction to professional training. Similarly many pre-medical courses, which deans of medical schools denounce in words but often favor in practice, are as illiberal as any study could be.

To some extent these deviations from the liberal concept arise from readiness to adopt as the college motto "the customer is always right." They arise from fear that enrollments will not grow, or a dread lest the maintenance of the integrity of the program will have an adverse effect upon the budget. They often reflect the unwillingness of the public relations department to promote what ought to be on the shelves; instead it exerts pressure to stock "what the public wants."

We know there is one way to prevent Gresham's law from operating in the field of public finance: it is to cling firmly to a policy of sound money. Such a policy vigilantly pursued never gives the law an opportunity to function. Precisely the same cure is applicable to college policy. An undiluted, simon-pure liberal arts curriculum will probably not bring many candidates for All-American nominations; assuredly the institution will never make a concealed profit (much less an open profit) from student fees; it may well be the college will not grow in size so fast as some of its neighbors. But it will be in a position to short-circuit completely the erosive effects of an academic Gresham's law.

One of the most important duties of the college is to

develop, and to challenge, the student's self-confidence. The liberal arts have suffered from lack of faith in their validity for the modern world. After all, students determine the content of their own education; of two students of equal capacity in the same course, one may enter upon it with zest and develop a deep and abiding interest; the other may go through the appropriate motions and purge himself of all knowledge as soon as the examination is over.

That mythical man, "the average student," has been damaged, I believe, not so much by the economic collapse of the thirties as by the resultant impairment of faith in the American system—economic, social, and political— which accompanied and has perpetuated that disaster. The mere monetary and production damages have long since been compensated. But the psychological effect has been a generation defensive in its mood about the economy in general and about its own economic viability in particular.

One has only to listen to the politicians at election time or to labor and industrial leaders at any time to hear the strong overtones of doubt as to the viability of our economy. The moment there is a hint of recession, there is an instant demand for make-work projects. In the course of the early part of 1954 there was an almost hysterical outburst of doubt that our economy would be prosperous if war contracts were cut back. We are dealing with a generation of students who were born in depression, grew up in wartime, and who only now find the world without a major military struggle. Even today our economy is heavily influenced by war production and war debts.

Through all their lives students have heard one word more often than any other, more often than "peace," more often than "strength"; the key word of this generation has been "security." Nearly all the great foundations for medical research in special fields have devoted themselves to scaring the people to death, even those who did not have their assorted diseases. The morning news comes with a catalogue of ills long enough to make a hypochondriac out of a robust Christian Scientist. No one has yet written a song on the theme, "Accentuate the negative," but the practice has been assiduously followed.

That is why many students come to college afraid of the word "culture," eager for skills, the more obviously marketable the better. That is why the liberal arts have staggered, why those who should have the profoundest faith in their validity nonetheless attach labels to them to make them seem "practical."

I hope this discussion has stressed the fact that there are many trends in the liberal arts at mid-century, some moving in favorable directions and others adverse to the studies appropriate to a free man. There are currents and eddies and, if one looks at the problem too narrowly, it may seem completely confused. Nonetheless, I think there is reason for optimism. We have emerged from depression and from war. We have made an economic readjustment without the catastrophic repercussions abroad which had been so freely predicted and without desperate measures at home. There are those who are terrified by Communism, but there are more who have faith that the democratic thesis is correct, that it will be vindicated. Industry is turning its resources, for the first time, to the support of the liberal arts, and the concept itself has been enlarged and refreshed. In my judgment, therefore, the dominant omens are favorable.

III ✒ Educating the Alumni
about Education

W HAT I am going to say should be regarded as reflections upon my own experiences in the field of alumni relations.

I was appointed publicity director, under what title I cannot recall, at the end of my sophomore year. The college, at that time, had no alumni secretary, no fund raising organization. Indeed, it had no dean, but a secretary of the faculty; the business officer was the librarian in his spare time—or vice versa. There was only a single stenographer, whose services were shared by the president, the secretary of the faculty—and me! Perhaps you will regard that situation as primitive—but at least you will admit that I was in on the ground floor. And I gained experience, for I had charge of publicizing the inauguration of a new president, which was attended by the President and the Vice President of the United States, and the Senator from New York who had been Secretary of War and Secretary of State. Of course, two or three days before the great event an alumnus came in and "directed" me!

American Alumni Council, District One Conference, Brown University, January 3, 1955

A decade later I served for a brief time as alumni secretary. For some years thereafter I was intimately connected with the work of that office. It included, in those far-off days, editing the magazine.

While a faculty member, I was given leave to run an endowment campaign for the then astronomical sum of three million dollars. Though that episode in my life is more than 30 years back, I never get over the realization that there has been less significant change in the design of that activity than any other connected with the college. The fund raising of the earlier twenties set a basic pattern; there have been refinements and gadgets, but no fundamental changes.

After reflecting upon these experiences, I reread many of the talks I have given upon alumni matters during the almost 30 years as a college president. Let me reassure you: this is not to be a digest of all those. I found that there had been some sharp changes in my attitudes, partly reflecting altered circumstances as work among alumni has come to much greater maturity. The changes were also partly due to the different perspective of greater age and longer experience upon my own part. Nonetheless, the fundamental theme, which grew out of my own contact with alumni work as a very young man, has persisted.

The time to start educating the alumni on the subject of education is before they ever get to college. The chances of making a good alumnus are immensely improved if the boy or girl goes to the right college—the one which can serve him most effectively. College preparation and college work are not so nearly standardized as they were when I went to college. Today high school curricula are varied to a degree, and so are college offerings. The juncture of the right student with the proper college and course *for him* is by so much the more difficult.

The student who goes to the wrong place, takes the wrong course, or for other reasons is out of step with his needs will make a discontented alumnus. The admission office, and the alumni who work with it, determine at the inception of his course the kind of relationship that is going to exist later.

The next step in educating the alumnus must occur during his years as an undergraduate. I will not labor the point, with which you must all be familiar, that many a man gets a degree by meeting formal requirements without ever getting an education in the process. If he has not learned to read anything better than a textbook, or an assigned passage, it will be an accident if he becomes a reader later, or understands what we are talking about.

Even if he has acquired some marketable skill, the degree carrier who has no real education is likely always to be out of step. As the years run on, he is more and more disillusioned about what he "got out of college" and, by extension, what it does for his successors. In the effort to justify himself, perhaps unconsciously, he generalizes his own experience. He will jibe at "Phi Betes"—pointing to some who "don't make as much as I do," and to others who are, from his point of view, "screwballs."

After college, the next step is, in every contact with alumni, to talk about education before all else. If, over a considerable series of years, meetings are centered on the development of the idea of continuing education as a way of life, the insistence will bring results. It requires skill, as well as deep conviction, to discuss nothing that does not bear directly upon education as a living and expanding process, and the responsibility of the alumnus to see that his college keeps the faith. To indicate that such a course is difficult is no argument against it; the whole educative process is difficult. Its dividends are neither quick nor tangible—but they are real.

The need for this insistence I learned the hard way. One of my associates was the most prolific publicity man I ever knew. He could get space galore. Some of his feature stories went literally around the world. One was about Rainbeau Harry; it told of an old college rule that men students could not walk on the campus with the women except to hold an umbrella in the rain. Harry carried an umbrella every day, everywhere, so as never to miss a chance. Even the British printed it! Sadly I let him go. The publicity certainly "got the name of the college into the news columns," but seldom about education. An ice chapel? Certainly. A pretty co-ed? Undoubtedly. An educational experiment? No.

It is difficult to publicize education: it has no color, little novelty; it is not news. A panty raid is different; the newspapers promoted the craze with crusading zeal in the news columns and denounced the escapades with equal zest on the editorial page—thus getting the best of two worlds.

Sometimes, unless you give it away, you may have trouble inducing the alumni publication to say much about education. I am not critical of the editors; education is not a good circulation booster, and as long as large circulation is essential to a favorable advertising rate that will balance the publication budget, a great deal of attention must be paid to items that will enlarge circulation. Moreover, there is more than crass commercialism involved. Unless the circulation of the alumni magazine is large, a huge section of our most vital constituency does not get the college message at all.

Because of these inherent difficulties, and because I believe a college should hammer away at its educational theme, I have always believed in sending the magazine free to all alumni. The cost is high, perhaps the rewards are not mensurable, but both assertions are applicable to all education. I have faith that even financially the practice pays real dividends—faith, but no proof.

To carry the educational message the college should speak with single voice. Let the president and trustees enunciate policy, and the job is done. How simple that sounds! Far too simple; policy is not made that way, because policy is not pronouncement; it is action. For that reason the real—the operative—policy may be set by someone who is not supposed to have policy-making powers.

To illustrate: some years ago college promotional material for prospective students came out with a rash of cover girls at archery. I leave to intelligent inference their garb and the camera angles; we all know the real target of the archery. What institution originated the idea of such a cover? One that had dropped football as incompatible with high educational standards. One whose president was justly famous for his educational views; he preached the liberal arts in season and out, scorned all extra-curricular flummery. I am not suggesting any insincerity; the chances are overwhelming that, engrossed as he was in great ideas, he never saw this piece of promotion.

Nor am I suggesting the liberal arts should not be made

attractive—and the cover was all that. But even if you got by the cover, you would have found nothing about the liberal arts, indeed nothing about the intellectual life! The whole booklet was one glad, sweet extra-curricular song.

It is not in promotion alone that policy in action is determined far from the "front office." A number of years ago a new instructor made a courtesy call soon after he arrived in town. During our conversation I asked about his courses, and how he was planning to handle them. What he told me was startling. When he had finished I congratulated him, perhaps with slight irony, upon his success in reversing several well-considered library policies which had been in operation for some time.

I am suggesting that before being over-critical of the alumni and their capacity hospitably to absorb educational ideas, officers and faculty should devote more time and thought to educating everyone on the campus about the integrity of the institution, the need to speak with one voice. However much they may discuss and debate the shape and fabric of policy within the walls, they should not contradict themselves in dealing with the alumni and the public.

Of course I do not mean that the alumni should hear of *nothing* but educational policy. That should be the main dish; they can have extra-curricular soup and athletic dessert. The essential thing is to maintain the right proportion. When persons from outside the college speak to major alumni groups, their theme should be relevant to its central idea. Travel talks, amusement, and many other perfectly respectable and proper topics belong elsewhere—to alumni as citizens or club members, but not as an alumni group gathered in the name of the institution, and preferably for its sake. If it is worth meeting for, it is worth hearing about.

Whenever I get a notice of a meeting which carries the promise, "there will be no solicitation of funds," I always want to stay away. This is not because I like to be dunned for money, since I have no more taste for that than the next man. The reasons I dislike it are that it constitutes a kind of confession about fund raising and carries a note of apology for expecting members of the college to support it. Most American fund raising consists of more or less skillfully contrived cries of agony. One of the fund raisers for a medical agency devoted to a single disease gave his formula for success: scare the living daylights out of them. You cannot scare the living daylights out of people by moaning about education; it does not strike home hard enough.

In any event, I think the technique is wrong for all purposes—even funds for specific diseases. So far as colleges are concerned, I am certain it is the wrong method. And one reason is that it contributes nothing to the "educational education" of the alumni. The "no solicitation at the dinner" notice is conclusive evidence of these things. All college fund raising should accentuate the positive— eliminate the negative—"don't mess with Mister In-between." Only by showing the *opportunity* can giving become a positive factor in alumni understanding.

The central point to stress is the faculty. A faculty may be defined as that which one appreciates only in retrospect. This is not characteristic of the American alumnus alone; Kipling expressed it for all men in his poem about his school days:

"Let us now praise famous men"—
Men of little showing—
For their work continueth,
And their work continueth,
Greater than their knowing.

And we all praise famous men—
Ancients of the College;
For they taught us common sense—
Tried to teach us common sense—
Truth and God's Own Common Sense
Which is more than knowledge!

Bless and praise we famous men—
Men of little showing!
For their work continueth
And their work continueth
Broad and deep continueth
Great beyond their knowing!

I have in my private office here at Brown three pictures: one, a gift and retained for historical reasons; second, a reproduction of a work of art which perpetually charms me for its sensitiveness, simplicity, and its insight into character; third, directly before my eyes, a photograph of a chapel door with three senior professors, who were deeply associated with my education, leaving the building for the last time together. One who nearly 40 years later retains as part of his intimate life such a picture cannot be accused of forgetting the teachers of his day. To most of the graduates of that college, however, those three men are scarcely names and of them they have no remembrance.

There is a constant tendency for alumni to assume that the current faculty does not have the grace, the learning, or the skill of those they knew. This is quite human, for it is in the sixth chapter of Genesis that the phrase appears, "There were giants . . . in those days." As I reflect upon my own college professors, beside the great ones, such as appear in my picture, were others who were trivial in their criticisms, sterile in their teaching, and inane in their jokes. In one class the text had been written by the professor who taught it. My dog-eared copy, acquired from Hinds and Noble, had each joke endorsed in the margin by some previous owner or, more likely, owners; they were even timed within the hour. With one of those manifestations of sadism of which students are often guilty, by prearrangement, we all laughed uproariously the moment he started the joke and stopped laughing just before he came to its presumed point. Only in the purple haze of anecdotage do such teachers assume a stature much greater than life.

We have to break through all this sentimentality by calling to the attention of our alumni those who now serve on faculties. We must dramatize them as people; we must direct attention to them as teachers, report on their scholarship, and try to give them, in the minds of alumni, that humane quality which endeared to us the men who taught us—particularly in retrospect.

In attempting this, we must resign ourselves to getting no help—or almost none—from the faculty members themselves. They are not in the publicity business; they see the extravagances of Madison Avenue and are fearful of being involved in a non-professional way. Scholars are wary of publicity and shy away from efforts to "popularize" them. I learned that lesson when I was a college fund raiser. I sought to prepare and publish what was then known as a "graphic," a kind of precursor to *Life* magazine—mostly pictures with some text. Inasmuch as faculty salaries were to be the principal objective of the fund raising drive, I wanted the graphic to feature the faculty. The episode occurred 35 years ago, but there lives in my memory the struggle, the argument, the pleading, the persuasion which produced what seemed to me then, and looks to me now, like a meager result.

Nevertheless, reflecting upon it in retrospect, I am deeply convinced that it was the right thing to do. Of course, it needed to be done with more skill and address, with more subtlety than a young and inexperienced man could command. But, after all, it was one of the earliest efforts to make the worth of a faculty the focal issue in an endowment campaign for what then seemed like an incredible sum of money, three million dollars. To all of you and all of us who seek to tell the alumni about the educational aspect of the college, the problem of presenting the faculty in right perspective is still central.

We have now to face the difficulty from another angle. Fear that faculties are radical has resulted largely from the failure of colleges and universities to present them in the right light to the public and the steady loss of confidence in the viability of democracy upon the part of some "patriots." This is a phase of the resistance to change of which I shall speak in a moment.

Meantime, there are segments of the public that have developed a passionate interest in what the student is told and what he reads. This is based upon an assumption, contrary to fact, that what leaves the professor is what enters the boy. If some of the people who harbor this naive idea were condemned to read 10,000, or even 100, examination papers, they would be quickly cured of this fantasy. When one depends, therefore, upon what some student says the professor said, he is on slippery ground. When he sees passages excerpted from books, out of context, and does not carefully analyze what else the student has read, he is more likely to be misled than to be instructed.

Those of us who are deeply concerned know all this. We know that the faculty represents a fairly wide spectrum of opinion and that the student is exposed not only to a variety of views, but to contrasting views. We know that if his reading is worth doing it involves still other points of view. What the student is told in one classroom or what he reads in one book is no measure of what the shape of his thoughts will be. Moreover, the atmosphere in which he lives, the habits he forms, the exchange of views with his associates—all these things are of profound importance.

I would not conceal the fact that there is a dangerous dislocation of faculty members from the economic system. They suffer when there is depression; they do not profit when there is inflation. They are, therefore, always on the adverse side of the economy, and every effort ought to be made to have their salaries reflect the prosperity of America, which they certainly do not as yet. However, anyone who has lived among them as long as I have knows that the danger from their adverse economic position is not radicalism; the danger is loss of zest, enthusiasm, and drive in their teaching.

Part of the misunderstanding by alumni arises from forgetfulness of their own youthful deviations from what they now regard as sanity. I remember well one very good trustee who used to harry me about the economics teaching. I stoutly defended the faculty without changing his mind. One day I learned that, as an undergraduate, he had been an ardent disciple of Henry George and had been, therefore, a single taxer. The next time he came to me with his complaints, I reminded him of this earlier economic view and asked him when he changed it. With the first glint of humor I had ever seen in a discussion of economics, he said, "When I bought my first piece of property." I never had to argue with him again. The student who never shocks his parents with his views is leading an abnormal life. To blame the faculty for this tension between the ages, which is as old as the time of man, is nonsense.

This leads directly to the fact that we must convince the alumni, if they are to understand the educational program, that change is not only inevitable, it is essential. We can do this by calling attention to the fact that the college is not a structure, it is an organism. It has a kind of basal metabolism without which life could not go on. Continuous change is a vital part of life, and once it stops the result is the death of an institution, as of an individual. If that thought becomes firmly implanted in the minds of the alumni, they will be more ready to accept change instead of nostalgically wanting to think in terms of the pump on the campus. If you asked them to conduct their business in the way it was done 20 years ago, they would instantly say that times have changed.

Surely, they have changed for education. The raw material which we take in is constantly changing, and the rapid transformation of primary, grammar, junior high and senior high school systems has not paused. The graduate schools are changing their methods and making different demands, as are the professional schools. The world of business, the world of politics, the world of religion, and even the world of culture are calling upon us to meet new situations, and it would be tragic if we learned no more about our job than our fathers knew.

Just as the accumulated knowledge of the physicist has made possible the transformation of the crude wireless into the richness of the best broadcasting, so educational experience, as it accumulates, points the way to improvements and refinements. We cannot restrict the subjects we teach to those which used to be taught, because the growth of knowledge has been so rapid and overwhelming that we face new problems in synthesis, from which we could not escape if we would. The physics I was taught is obsolete; so also are the sociology, the psychology, and even much of the history, for when I learned history one of the books that most profoundly interested me was Sir John R. Seeley's *The Expansion of England,* which made imperialism respectable. In my college days I used to adore hearing H. Morse Stephens read the poetry of Rudyard Kipling, the apostle of imperialism.

> *"Boots—boots—boots—boots—movin' up and down again!*
> *There's no discharge in the war!"*

In short, there are deep and moving tides in education; we have to admit there are also surface chops. Our programs have often been bedeviled by the wind-blown spume. There has been too much curricular "gadgetting," which hid the fundamental reforms. Many administrators have rushed from one gaudy episode to another, calling them "experiments" when they were really nothing but publicity tricks. I shall not defend these, but they can be discounted as ephemeral. If you cast your minds back, you will notice that they had their brief day and disappeared.

The deeper moving tides we resist at our peril. There was a time when all science was "natural philosophy," when political economy covered a whole range of departments; to pretend that one can now subsume all modern developments under the old labels is to put new wine into old bottles with the inevitable rupture the Bible described.

The alumni tend to be conservative, and I would not have it otherwise, but they must mediate between the new and the old in order to bind together every segment into one constituency. We insist that they appreciate the fact that the true conservative is of necessity a reformer. England had a phrase which revealed this: "Tory Democracy." The designation was inaccurate, but suggestive. The person who seeks to prevent reform is a reactionary, not a conservative; and a reactionary denies the dynamics of history. He makes Mrs. Partington, sweeping back the tide with her broom, or Canute, asking the seas to halt, look like sane and constructive people.

The importance of this cannot be over-stated, for the function of the professional educator is analogous to that of an architect; the owner can accept or reject what the architect plans. Some buildings have been greatly improved because of the critical attitude of the owner, but many another has been impaired or destroyed by his lack of taste or knowledge. In education, as in architecture or almost anything else, the amateur is ultimately the master of the professional as, of course, he must be, if democracy is to achieve its destiny. The alumnus will accept or reject our educational designs; the indoctrination of alumni in the inevitability of change is fundamental.

I have but one other observation to make. Should we be impatient that progress in these matters has been so slow? I believe not. Perhaps it is my training as a historian that shapes my view, but, in the long perspective of the history of the American college, alumni organization, at least in its modern form, is relatively new. Furthermore, alumni activity was not undertaken upon the initiative of the colleges; it was the alumni themselves who organized, and then began to offer advice or service or both.

Their initiative was somewhat ungraciously regarded both by the trustees and by administrative officers. This arose partly because some of their views were bumptiously expressed, but much more because the structure of the American college was already exceedingly complex. Nowhere else in the world is there the tripartite structure of the faculty, the trustees, and the administration that exists here. The effort to integrate a fourth body, the organized alumni, into what was already not only complex, but clumsy, seemed well nigh hopeless.

Only slowly did the idea of capitalizing upon the enthusiasm and sentimental attachment of alumni dawn upon the officers who were distraught by their search for money. It was only when the money angle began to be important that the alumni were given representation upon boards of trustees. Even then, the integration of alumni with the structure or control was deficient and, when they sought to use financial leverage, the results were distressing. It was this which led a former Brown instructor, Percy Marks, to coin the expression "pestiferous alumni." It was this, also, which led a famous university administrator to assert that universities "are restrained by the enormous power of organized alumni, who are at best conservative and at the worst out and out reactionary."

I have never shared these views. Perhaps my early relationship to publicity, to alumni organizations, and to fund raising led me to see the other side of the shield. Insofar as there have been friction and disharmony, I believe that they arose from the failure to make alumni feel that they are members of the college. They were allowed activity divorced from responsibility, and that is always a disastrous separation. It is as we make headway in expounding the educational aims of the college, as we make real the integration of the alumni organization into the fabric of its management that we can bring to bear every strength essential to the task which educational institutions face.

PART II ☞ *Brown*

IV ✐ Installation

FELLOW Members of the Family of Brown University:
I speak to you no longer as an alien and a stranger.
By this ceremony of adoption just now completed I have
entered into your heritage and have become one of the
co-heirs of your traditions and achievements, joint tenant
of your properties and purposes, co-worker in the fulfillment of your duties and obligations, fellow exponent
of your ideals.

One does not enter upon this post of potential leadership with any feeling of pride. The sense of responsibility
is sufficiently daunting to make any such temper not only
inappropriate but impossible. Rather one comes into
such a succession with a sense of deep humility.

Humility should not be confused with timidity. The
great exemplar of humility was bold in driving the money-
changers from the temple, in denouncing the Scribes and
Pharisees. He was bolder yet in establishing a design for
living never perfectly realized, save in His own life, but
still the most wonderful ethical pattern known to men.
Boldness, therefore, must march with humility in the
search for a full and rich interpretation of the destiny of
this institution.

Brown University, February 3, 1937

Historically, it is safe to say, Brown has exercised its most significant influence when its progress was most courageous. Boldness was manifest in the very organization of the University. I have read the Charter many times, each time with a growing sense of admiration for the foresight and the faith of those who, in that distant past, set an objective which is as valid today as it was then, and explained the bases with words which have never needed to be revised. It is still the purpose of a liberal education to form "the rising generation to virtue, knowledge, and useful literature" and thus preserve "in the community a succession of men duly qualified for discharging the offices of life with usefulness and reputation."

That enterprise was in perfect accord with the spirit of the colonial Charter; for education is indeed "a lively experiment." Those words have peculiar significance for such an institution as this. "Lively" does not mean mere restlessness; it does not refer to nervous and unstable activity. In the way in which the word was used in those days, it carried the fine and rich connotation of life itself, for all living is an experiment. In accord with that ideal we should seek to make this University a lively manifestation of the search for new truths, for finer interpretations, for fresh insights, and richer emotional responses.

I would not have us confine the life of the University within the boundaries of some formal plan. Plans in education are an attempt to transfer the ideas of the engineer to a realm for which they are not well adapted. College plans are usually mechanical in design and are imposed as alien elements upon foundations which they do not fit. Though we should not have a plan of that kind, we must continue to develop distinctive characteristics which express with vigor and with intelligence the individual personality of this University.

Its personality can best find expression through the association of two societies: the first composed of competent scholars working freely, each in the medium best adapted to his capacities, his tastes, and his intellectual interests; the second, energetic and active youth, learning freely and responsibly along with their more experienced teachers. It is the function of the administrative officers to keep open the channels of teaching and of learning for the faculty and for the students.

When Brown University was founded, and for a century thereafter, it was the only institution of higher education in Rhode Island and Providence Plantations. With the expanding needs of the commonwealth and changing demands, it was not only proper but necessary that other institutions should be called into being to share our responsibilities. This University was not designed as a monopoly. Therefore, far from regretting the development of other institutions of higher education. we welcome the cooperation of these younger colleagues. We do not seek an exclusive position; rather, we seek to achieve a distinguished place in the life of our city and state—and in the nation.

Religious freedom and spiritual progress were linked in the Charter, as they have always been in human experience. In other aspects of life, also, freedom and progress belong together. If the universities of today preserve and reinterpret that inheritance of freedom, now selling at so disastrous a discount in the political and social markets of the world, they will make an important contribution to the present and the future.

One phrase in the Charter is set higher than any other.

After the statement of objectives, after the provision for administration, and after that magnificent passage about religious freedom, occurs the phrase, "Above all,"—that is, beyond everything else—" a constant regard [is to] be paid to, and effectual care taken of, the morals of the College." That passage seems to me a brilliant jewel in an unusually brilliant Charter.

The world today is not so much in need of skill as of character. We do not lack ability so much as we lack purpose. Our capacity for achievement in public life and in private life tends to outrun our ethical impulses. Let us make Brown University an exponent of a way of life which is intellectually alert, which is aesthetically and emotionally sensitive, and which is spiritually vigorous.

V ✍ The Years Look Down

W E HAVE NOT had an occasion of this magnitude for the opening of a building at Brown University for nearly 30 years. Yet several of our most important structures have been erected during that period. It is precisely because University Hall is old, rather than new, that we rejoice. This is its fifth major construction enterprise.

One hundred and seventy years ago on March 27 spades were set to the ground, and on May 14, 1770, John Brown laid the first foundation stone at the southwest corner on land once owned by his great-great-grandfather, Chad Brown, "the original proprietor after the native Indians of whom it was purchased." The situation was "exceedingly pleasant and healthy, being on the summit of a hill the ascent easy and gradual, commanding an extensive prospect of hills, dales, plains, woods, water, islands, etc." No wonder it was called a spot "made for a seat of the Muses." The construction of frame and walls was swift under the energetic direction of the contributed services of the brothers Brown, and the cost less than $10,000. Yet James Manning called the building "elegant" and "beautiful," and its size was tremendous, "near

Rededication of University Hall, Brown University, May 4, 1940

as large as Babel" to *The Boston Gazette.*
We know little of the original interior finish. Indeed, it
was slow in getting any at all. In November, 1771, only
five or six of the rooms on the first floor were finished off,
and none was occupied by students. During the winter of
1771-1772 the first two floors were finished, but the third
waited until 1785 and the top story till 1788. Even the
roof had a temporary covering while money for slate was
being collected. No cupola was built until 1791 when a
newly acquired bell called for an efficient housing.

Before the building was fully completed and occupied
by the infant college, it was taken away from the control
of the Corporation. Founded just after the close of the
French and Indian War, the institution had never seen
peaceful times, or freedom from political disturbances.
Commencement programs reflected the growing tension
until the Class of 1775 omitted their public commencement exercises because of "the distresses of our oppressed
country." President Manning foresaw that "institutions of
learning will doubtless partake in the common calamities
of our country, as arms have ever proved unfriendly to
the more refined and liberal arts and sciences." Within a
year his prediction was fulfilled and he wrote: "The royal
army landed in Rhode Island and took possession [of
Newport]. . . . This brought their camp in plain view from
the College with the naked eye; upon which the country
flew to arms and marched for Providence; there, unpro-
vided with barracks they marched into the College and
dispossessed the students, about 40 in number."

The American troops occupied the building from December 7, 1776, until April 20, 1780. Instantly upon its
evacuation Manning planned to reopen the edifice for
college use, but on May 5, 1780, Governor Greene noti-

fied him that it was under consideration as a hospital "for the reception of the French invalids." On June 25, the building was "seized" and served that purpose until May 27, 1782.

The discipline of the patriot army was not its most notable characteristic. Manning spoke of the "rude and wasting soldiery," and of the "great waste and destruction . . . made . . . by men whose profession has destruction for its object."

When the edifice was diverted to use as a hospital, the new tenants "made great alterations in the building, highly injurious to the designs of its founders." Auxiliary structures were built and the walls breached to provide access. "Many of the windows are also taken entirely out of the house, and others so broken, as well as the slate on the roof, that storms naturally beat into it." We gain some insight into hospital conditions, as well as the state of the building, by Manning's lament when at last it was returned: "The Corporation have ordered the augean stable cleansed. . . . It is left in a most horrid, dirty, shattered situation." Indeed, the French asserted that they had repaired the building when they took it over, and set "about knocking down the closets . . . to sell the boards"; they also planned to "sell all the college windows . . . and say that they put them all in, and of course they belong to the King."

Nothing daunted, the Corporation hired the money to put the building in some shape and set about the heartbreaking task of attempting to collect damages—a process that continued for 18 years. After the first three years of futile effort it was suggested that western land would be accepted in compensation, since its ultimate sale might bring the desired cash. In the effort to secure redress

Manning even accepted an appointment by the General Assembly in March, 1786, to the Congress of the Confederation. His hope to gain consideration of the claims of the College from that bankrupt body was frustrated, and he resigned—a resignation embittered by the refusal of the General Assembly to pay his salary in anything but depreciated paper currency.

After the new Constitution was adopted and Rhode Island adhered, the attempt was renewed. By 1795 Alexander Hamilton reported: "It is the opinion of the Secretary [of the Treasury] . . . that in this, and all similar cases, affecting the interests of literature, indemnification and compensation ought to be made." Not until three years later did the Committee on Claims report favorably to the House of Representatives, but nothing happened. At last, in March, 1800, a new report was acted upon. An attempt was made to include the damages caused by its use as a hospital, but that proposal was rejected on the ground that our allies "were to procure their own supplies, and pay for their own damages." Even with that amendment eliminated, the bill received only a tie vote, which the Speaker of the House resolved in favor of the College. John Adams signed the bill on April 18, 1800, and finally the Corporation, which had asked £2300, received $2,779.13.

No claims were ever presented to the King of France though his patronage through the establishment of a chair of French history and literature was invited. This was partly in discharge of the eternal obligation of the Corporation and its officers to solicit funds for this literary, although eleemosynary, enterprise. But it was done also because French officers had been quartered with several members of the Corporation and other prominent citi-

zens, and had aroused a lively interest, which other benefits, military and pecuniary, of the alliance had accentu-
ated. Benjamin Franklin, and later Thomas Jefferson,
when he succeeded as Minister to France, quietly declined
to transmit the request.

The repairs after the Revolution were so extensive as
to constitute a major reconstruction. Thereafter the building was in service without notable change until 1834.
By that time it was in bad condition. Students were
not nearly so orderly then as they are today. The damage
they did was exceedingly severe. One student wrote,
"The entries nightly resound with crashing of bottles
and the hoarse rumbling of wood and stones." Nor
was the maintenance department very fully developed.
When Manning Hall was built, 12 years after Hope
College, the old edifice was inspected by a committee of
the Corporation, which reported it had "arrived at that
state of decay that very considerable repair is necessary
to prevent it from going to entire destruction. The win-
dow frames must be taken out. . . . The bricks should be
painted or covered with cement—the mortar has come
out from between the bricks. Many of the bricks are
much decayed." Moreover, styles had changed. The
classic revival, exemplified in its pure form in Manning
Hall, and later less satisfactorily in Rhode Island, led men
no longer to look upon University Hall as either "beautiful" or "elegant," and it was thought a coat of cement
would improve its appearance. At that time the balustrade
around the roof was removed and the old bell replaced
by the one now in use.

Before the middle of the century the building was again
given over to soldiery. The stormy political life of Rhode
Island had one of its most dramatic crises in the Dorr

Rebellion. Troops poured into Providence, and on June 25, 1842, at the request of the Executive Council, University Hall was appropriated to their use for several days.

In 1850 minor changes were made in the original structure. The erection of Manning Hall had provided a new chapel and released for other uses the former chapel which occupied the first two stories in the west projection. Consequently, a floor was laid in place of the balcony, and the lower and upper rooms became classrooms. The east projection had a large room on the first floor which had served as a college commons. It was a perpetual source of irritation, uproar, and damage to property, and was then abandoned. That space also was converted to classroom purposes. Ten years later the long hallways were partitioned at intervals. These changes were made with an eye to the practical, rather than the aesthetic, and we need have no regrets at their subsequent disappearance.

Within 20 years the necessity for another general renovation was acute. President Robinson spoke with vigor of the shocking condition of University Hall. "Its battered doors, its defaced walls, the gaping flooring of its hallways, and the unmistakable odor of decay pervading the building" proclaimed its needs. "Both within and without [it was] an eyesore and a reproach." One of the elder members of the Corporation who lived in the building at this time has told me that on more than one occasion when he wished to build a fire he knocked some more plaster from the gaping holes and tore off the lath beneath for use as kindling. Its "entries and doorways . . . had never been lighted at night; the students groped their way up and down as best they could." The stairways, which ran north and south in the hallways, were made of hewn logs, and over a century of traffic had grooved them so that in the center they made substantially an inclined plane.

"The loud demand of many friends of the College was to level it to the ground, and to put up a modern structure in its place." In this view the students apparently joined, for an editorial in *The Brunonian* declared: "University Hall . . . has nobly served several generations, and it is impossible to find anything connected with the building which is not more or less impaired by time both as respects its appearance and usefulness; its halls are dark, and it is low-studded, inconvenient and dirty; defects which it seems impossible to remedy by any means short of entire demolition. The fact that it is a relic of the past, and endeared by many pleasant associations may be an argument for allowing it to stand, in the opinion of antiquarians and graduates of fifty years ago, but can have but little weight to the rising generation of students who know the discomfort of rooming within its hoary walls. . . . University Hall patched up, would only half satisfy any one; a new University Hall would be a source of pride and pleasure to both officers and students for many years."

However, the Corporation appointed a committee in June, 1880, "to procure plans and estimates for the reconstruction of University Hall," and it was "continued for the purpose of securing the necessary funds." The actual work was perhaps hastened by a smoldering fire between the ceiling and floor of two classrooms in the south section in January, 1882. More damage was done by the enthusiastic axes of the students and their energy in suppressing it than by the fire itself.

After three years' consideration, and the raising of $50,000, much the same sort of operation was performed as that now completed. The entire inside of the building was removed and replaced with new material, and a new roof put on the old frame. New stairways were built, crowded inconveniently into the entry spaces. The recitation rooms, which had occupied the space of chapel and commons, gave place to a couple of large, two-story rooms, each with a gallery. The floor space of each was greater than the old chapel or commons because the hallway which had separated those rooms was divided between the new ones. Steam heat and gas light were provided, and running water. To make room for the heater, and toilet rooms, the basement was deepened. However, the walls were not properly underpinned, but merely buttressed with rubble on the inside. This allowed the use of the additional space in the basement, although it imperiled the security of the building.

At this same time windows regarded as modern were substituted for those with small panes; the design selected would now be considered about the worst possible. The appearance was made still worse because students exercised their own taste in blinds and shutters. Some windows had one sort of cover, others different types, and some none at all. Also the chimneys were rebuilt to conform more nearly with those of Slater, with a maximum of falsework and decoration; the cupola was encased, giving it a much heavier and lower appearance; and the balustrade around the roof was replaced. The cement coating was left as it was, but "painted of a neutral olive tint." The expense of the reconstruction was five times the original cost of the building. Some of it, particularly in the two large rooms, was handsomely done, but in general its emphasis was on plain, and unhappily rather ugly, utility. At that moment the design of doors and windows and woodwork was at a singularly low ebb, and the results have remained all too apparent for over a half a century.

The changing tastes in architecture were reflected once again when the beauty of the colonial was rediscovered. In 1905 the cement casing on University Hall was carefully removed from the old brick, the "modern" windows were taken out and replaced with small panes, the chimneys were put back into form more nearly approaching the first ones, and the belfry retouched. So far as the exterior was concerned, the building stood again as originally designed, and its dignity has since been recognized more and more fully.

The external "beauty" having been restored in 1905, the present reconstruction seeks to give the interior the "elegance" of which President Manning spoke. It is a good word; it does not signify something elaborate, but suggests restrained and simple dignity. We have left everything that remained of the original building except some concealed timbers of the old belfry. Even the old roof timbers are still in place, protected so far as possible by an automatic sprinkler system. The rubble which inadequately braced the old foundations has been taken out, and the walls have had new foundations set beneath them. The new frame, which is of steel and concrete, is hidden by materials more appropriate to a structure of this kind. The windows now installed are either the sixth or seventh set to be put in the old brickwork. The large rooms in the east and west projections approximate the early chapel and commons more nearly than their predecessors.

Truly the architecture of University Hall tells a characteristic story. For old as it is, it meets the demands of the modernists. It is as "functional" as any building one could find. There are no useless ornaments, it is not loaded with fussy and meaningless detail. Indeed, the belfry remained unbuilt until there was a bell to swing, and was as spare as it could be and still discharge its function. The building depends for its beauty upon admirable proportions, upon cleanness of line, upon effective masses, upon the color and texture of its surface. It was dedicated to light. Not until the windows were taken out did the amount of wall space devoted to windows come into the focus of attention. Among colonial structures it is all but unique in the proportion of surface given over to light. As it met the standards of a far-off day, so also it meets our own.

All the vicissitudes through which University Hall has passed are worthy of note, because, in this day, it is well to recall the French maxim, "the more things change, the more they remain the same." The building was erected as the heart of the College, and so it has remained for 170 years. When it was built free institutions were threatened, and they are still in jeopardy. This is a moment of anxiety over liberty and its blessings. Democracy is on trial for its life both here and abroad. The history of this building, what has been said and done here in war and in peace, in public and in private, remind us that it has ever been so.

The College was founded on the morrow of a world war, and saw no settled peace during the first 50 years of its history. Soon after it opened the colonial governor was dismissed for assaulting the liberties of the people. The "Gaspee" was burned, the tea was destroyed, the Revolution was fought for liberty. The freedom of the seas, so vital to this port, was destroyed by the embargo, fought for in 1811—and slowly won, only to be surrendered again. Dorr's Rebellion was a footnote in the great history of the struggle for our freedom—and the Civil War a glowing chapter. University Hall has thrice been occupied by troops. The college was denuded of students in one war and its attendance greatly affected during four others. As we again look out upon a world at war, the history which this old building has witnessed suggests we take the long view and curb our pessimism upon the one hand and our wishful, utopian dreams upon the other. "Eternal vigilance is the price of liberty"—and the last 170 years have shown that again and again.

The college edifice once looked over hills and valleys, fields and woods, rivers and the bay with its islands. Its outlook in the physical sense is now more confined, but its prospect runs beyond the power of the eye alone. The seaport, ruined by British occupation in the Revolution, ruined by the embargo in the days of Jefferson, ruined again by the War of 1812, ruined by tidal waves and catastrophes has each time shown powers of recuperation and growth that should give us heart. Exhaustion, poverty, disaster are events of the moment, but life is renewed by changing seasons and by changing generations. If we can no longer see the fields and woods, we have crowded about us the evidences of the growth of a community. And the college still stands at the center of that life; it is still its most distinguished asset.

While University Hall is indeed part of the life of this nation, it belongs most intimately to this city and this commonwealth. For it was designed by local men, its bricks were from nearby Rehoboth, its artisans were from Providence and Boston. The original cost, and the costs of its successive regenerations, have been met by the philanthropic generosity of the local citizenry. Because of its intimate association with this commonwealth, it is most appropriate to have the Governor here to bring the greetings of the State.

VI ✍ University Architecture

THERE has been some public discussion and a rising tide of interest in our architectural problems. The publication of the campaign booklet, *A Home for the Liberal Ideal,* was in general greeted with enthusiasm, but in some quarters it was felt that we should build in a more "modern" style. Construction of Whitehall, on the other hand, has aroused feelings that we have departed from an established architectural pattern. If we look at our problems in broader terms than the immediate, we can think about them more constructively.

No action of the Corporation ever established any given style for new buildings. President Faunce, in his report of October, 1901, said it was "necessary to have some definite plan for the architectural future of Brown. Our present buildings were obviously erected without any reference to a general scheme of development, and represent every period in architectural history. . . . This heterogeneousness, which we share with most New England colleges, is certainly picturesque, and the *ensemble,* softened by time, is not unpleasing. But it is now time for some definite plan of architectural development."

Excerpt from the President's Report to the Corporation of Brown University, October 12, 1946

As a consequence Frederick Law Olmsted, the most distinguished man in the field at that time, made a general layout and Professor William R. Ware of Columbia University was appointed consulting architect. There were various consulting architects during succeeding years when Brown was engaged in numerous building enterprises. In 1903 Caswell Hall was erected and in the same year the Engineering Building, the Colgate-Hoyt Swimming Pool, and Rockefeller Hall which is now part of Faunce House. The John Carter Brown Library and Carrie Tower were built in 1904. The John Hay Library was constructed in 1910, Arnold Laboratory in 1915.

In September, 1903, President Faunce stated in his report: "We might conceivably have engaged a single firm of architects to plan all our new buildings, and so entrust our architectural future entirely to them. But for various reasons this proved impracticable. The result of having many buildings planned by a single brain would surely be harmonious, but it might also prove monotonous. We have adopted the alternative plan, of having various architects, all working in conference with one consulting architect and with one landscape gardner. . . . We trust the result will show a dominant motive in the choice of materials and the general design, together with the variety which befits structures intended for widely different uses."

By 1920 the Olmsted plan was obsolete and in October of that year President Faunce said: "We need now a policy to guide our physical development for the next half century. We cannot live from hand to mouth, purchasing a piece of ground because it is in the market, or locating a building or selecting a style of architecture because of the wishes of friends or donors. We must have a comprehensive plan, not indeed as a strait jacket, but as a 'pattern in the mount.' . . . Long ago, we decided that our architecture must henceforth conform in general to the Georgian or 'colonial' style, which not only reminds us of the age in which the University was founded, but is far better adapted than the Gothic to give the generous lighting needed in modern libraries and laboratories."

Thereupon, general plans for the expansion of the University were prepared by the late Paul Crèt and, save for the extension of Faunce House and the location of the Marvel Gymnasium, they have been followed with reasonable consistency. The Metcalf Research Laboratory was built precisely where his plans directed. Marston Hall and Whitehall are on ground reserved for classrooms. One of the new quadrangles is to go where he planned to have dormitories constructed in the quadrangle design.

There has been a feeling, as President Faunce stated, that the style should be what is sometimes called Georgian and sometimes called Colonial. But it is obvious that the style of University Hall and the "Georgian" of Metcalf Research Laboratory or Hegeman belong to different traditions, that Faunce House does not follow either tradition. Not many people would recognize the John Hay Library in the following official description: "The style is therefore Georgian, which corresponds to the colonial work in America, and is simple, reserved and dignified."

In point of fact, few institutions in the country have been as little dominated by architectural tradition as Brown. Our first building was true Colonial. The second, Hope College, showed a marked modification of ideas in the span of 53 years. And in the next 11 years there was a radical shift, for Manning Hall illustrates the Greek Revival in its purest form. The fourth building, Rhode

Island Hall, represented some degeneration of that idea. Rogers Hall set a new style.

The old library building (now Robinson Hall) took its inspiration from the Gothic. It was designed in what was then regarded as the most efficient form of library construction with the books grouped about a series of bays where the students could work in close contact with the volumes which they needed at the moment. In his report to the Corporation in June, 1878, President Robinson said: "The building, as now completed, gives universal satisfaction. Its location is most fitting; its architecture is both pleasing to the eye and congruous with the uses to which the structure is devoted; and its internal arrangements are all that can be desired, whether for the convenience of those who may wish to consult the library or of those who may be charged with the care of it."

Succeeding buildings—Slater, Sayles, Lyman, and Wilson—showed steady modifications of ideas. Maxcy was considered a thoroughly modern building when it was constructed. The John Hay Library represented a monumental concept in form, material, and setting. At the opposite end of the campus, Marston Hall brought still another type and style of architecture, with wholly different treatment and building material.

It must be remembered, too, that University Hall itself was for many years regarded as old fashioned and outmoded. This should be a reminder that tastes change and that what was once the pride of the early College, and is now again the pride of an old University, was for a half century or more held in contempt.

When, therefore, it is assumed that Brown has an established form of architecture from which it does not deviate and that the University is not open to ideas of design, nothing could be further from the truth. Indeed, it was said by a distinguished architect that he did not know another spot in the United States like our College Green where, standing in one place, a person could review, with appropriate examples, so much of the history of American architecture.

I should like to suggest what seems to me a sound basis for our policy. The matter should not be approached dogmatically or with slogans, clichés, and platitudes. We might just as well face the fact that there is more theology in modern architecture than in modern religion. We are presented with dogmas about what is modern and what is not modern which have no functional substance whatever. There are conventions as rigid and designs as imitative in the so-called modern as in the so-called traditional styles. Actually, much of the "modern" in America is transplanted from Germany; much certainly fails to adapt exterior to interior function, whatever that may mean to the professional or the layman. There are conventions about fenestration which have no relationship to the use of the structure or to the comfort and convenience of the workers inside. In matters of taste dogma is not very intelligent, and we should avoid being disconcerted by slogans, rigidities, and assertions.

The statement that we live in the twentieth century and therefore should not use an eighteenth century style is meaningless. University Hall represents, in many ways, our most modern building: from the standpoint of convenience and pure efficiency it is among our best. Where the most radical departures have been made in an attempt to follow current fashions, as in Maxcy, the John Hay Library, and Marston, the buildings have been subjected to the most acid criticism.

The core of our policy should be the careful consideration of all the factors involved. The function of a building
is important. In Whitehall, for example, it was determined
to have classrooms and nothing else. The building was
designed to accommodate a maximum number of classes
of given sizes with the greatest flexibility and the fullest
possible use.

Secondly, we should take account of what materials are
available. Whitehall again illustrates the point. It stands
next to a structure built of Indiana limestone and, other
things being equal, it might have been well to use Indiana
limestone for Whitehall. But from the standpoint of cost
and time of delivery it was impossible. Red brick would
not have harmonized with that particular environment;
moreover red brick would not have been available for
several months. White brick could be delivered promptly.
Metal sash like those of Marston could not have been acquired in time for use. Clear glass windows in close
proximity to Marston would mean a disturbing lack of
privacy to the occupants of both buildings, whereas glass
brick would give a maximum of illumination in Whitehall
and more reflected light for the north side of Marston; and
glass brick was available. It goes without saying that white
brick and glass brick do not lend themselves to colonial
treatment or Georgian design and therefore the architectural style had to be adapted to the materials.

Thirdly, we should pay attention to surroundings. We
should not build in close juxtaposition structures which
are violently inharmonious in style. If too many styles of
architecture are crowded upon each other in a restricted
space, the result is infelicitous. Again we may use Whitehall as an illustration. If it had been set on the main campus its violently contrasting style would have been an

outrage. In the environment in which it is placed, it does not assault the sensibilities.

The last consideration should be decorative qualities. With regard to those little need be said. Our best buildings are those which depend upon harmony of proportion and simplicity of line for their effect and not upon meretricious and adventitious items.

The basic plan for the proposed quadrangle was founded upon the uses to which the buildings would be put, and the nature of the organizations and individuals who would occupy them. It was conditioned by the necessity for making really huge structures seem more intimate and less overpowering and of putting relatively vast buildings on severely restricted space and still preserving some sense of spaciousness. Those are not inconsiderable tasks. Many people have spoken of the way in which the College Green seems to have been enlarged and to have gained in spaciousness by the new arrangement of walks. The straight-line perspective between George and Waterman Streets has helped to create that impression; putting more greenery in front of University Hall has made it less crowded against the driveway. In much the same manner careful design of the quadrangle will make large buildings on small spaces look less crowded and less institutional.

VII ✒ Dedication of the Quadrangle

T ODAY symbolizes the end of the construction phase of a great effort. Before us is the materialization of the dreams of many—not alone of this generation, but of scores who went before.

For that reason various parts of the quadrangle are named for men who cherished the great aims of Brown— educators, scholars, statesmen, jurists, physicians, soldiers, and businessmen. Each in his own way fulfilled the promise—and the demand—of our ancient Charter. We have not sought to honor them; their lives were full of honor, as of achievement. The buildings and courts bear their names to remind oncoming generations that they enter upon a noble—and an enduring—heritage.

The inspiration goes back to President Wayland's epochal report to the Corporation of Brown University, and the quadrangle embodies the ideal which he stated with explicit clarity 100 years before the date incised on the weather vane over the tower of Wayland House. It is singularly appropriate, therefore, that the main entrance is through the building named for him and that the corner-stone for the whole project is set in its wall. Although he

Brown University, June 1, 1952. The Quadrangle was named for President Wriston by vote of the Corporation when he retired on August 16, 1955.

did not visualize structures of this size, or in this precise form, nonetheless the root idea was his, and virtually every successor has—with greater or less insistence and eloquence—advocated what now appears around us. Indeed, exactly 30 years ago a committee of the Corporation had plans prepared for a major housing development on this very site.

To give substance to the hopes of our fathers, we have levied upon the vision and skill of many contemporaries. In making ideas concrete, literally as well as figuratively, they have been made rigid; their present form fastens upon our successors any deficiencies in imagination, any errors of perception. As the years run on we must ask their indulgence on the ground that we have done our best. Nothing that generosity could provide or energy achieve or labor attain has been left undone. There have been economies, many of them painful, but no sacrifice of the fundamental idea.

For every gift which expressed love of learning and respect for the integrity of this University in its vital task, our heartfelt thanks. For every suggestion and insight which combined to make this the product of many minds, our warm appreciation. For every skill contributed by artisans, contractors, architects, and landscape designer, our deepest gratitude. Here is the union of heart and hand and brain—a vast cooperative effort of alumni and friends, volunteers and officers. That is the great achievement thus far.

But we cannot rest here, for in a larger sense the work is just begun. These buildings were constructed to facilitate a distinctive way of life. Certainly not since the first world war of the twentieth century have the officers and students of Brown University possessed adequate instruments for stimulating that way of life. Few here today have any experience in the use of such means for the attainment of that objective.

The goal of our endeavor is nothing strange or peculiar, much less unique. Francis Wayland's description may seem somewhat negative. We have assumed, he said, "the responsibility of a superintendence which we have rendered ourselves incapable of fulfilling" since "our buildings were constructed with no reference to this objective." As a consequence we "lost the humanizing effect produced by the daily association of students with older and well bred gentlemen, so obvious in an English college." Brown is not an English college, nor do we wish it to become one. Our colleges stem from England, but they have been transformed by the new environment and by characteristically American ideals and methods.

Nothing has transpired, however, which makes college teaching independent of the stimulation of immature minds by daily contact with more experienced, alert, and expanding intelligences. To that end members of the academic staff are to live in the dormitories as resident fellows. They will be neither proctors nor disciplinary officers, but exemplars of the scholar's way of life. It calls for profound dedication and arduous labor, but is in no degree inconsistent with an urbane, even a gay, experience. The fellows are also to be a manifestation of that central tenet of the liberal gospel—that it makes far less difference what a man does than what he becomes, for life consists in coming to terms with harsh reality without letting tragedy dominate one's thoughts or feelings.

I hope each resident fellow will surround himself with a group of other faculty members who will take informal and extra-curricular responsibility for the house to which he is attached. This will broaden the acquaintance between the faculty and students through contacts outside the classroom. It should help give an intellectual tone to social intercourse and create that humane atmosphere so essential to the growth of liberal ideals.

Each house should acquire characteristics of its own. They should develop informally as some thread of mutual activity becomes traditional, rather than through a written constitution or in any other stilted way. Hobbies such as photography or woodworking or modeling or some other outlet for energy and skill may provide an avenue to this goal.

The current world desperately needs a lively sense of craftsmanship. The capacity to entertain one's self and to develop an adequate foil to one's principal occupation is a great help to emotional stability in a neurotic age. Learned Hand has said that "among the most precious and dependable of our satisfactions is the joy of craftsmanship." Creative activity "gives us the sense of our own actuality, an escape from the effort to escape, a contentment that the mere stream of consciousness cannot bring, a direction, a solace, a power, a philosophy."

Houses might be encouraged to exhibit their work from time to time. That sort of thing cannot be useful if forced or artificial, but the quadrangle will assume a new dimension of meaning if extra-curricular cultural activities grow naturally, yet vigorously, under wise stimulation.

Each house should be a center of lively and rich social life. Those who are not members of fraternities must not lack opportunity for the kinds of experience which help raw freshmen grow into knowledgeable seniors.

All these suggestions recognize that, as Aristotle said so long ago, man is a social animal. College boys are at the most gregarious age. But these buildings will fail of their purpose and the elaborate care which has been taken to give each room four very solid walls, cushioned floors, and quiet ceilings will have been wasted unless there is also an opportunity for the student to spend some time alone.

Today there is continuous talk about the necessity for developing toleration, but there is far too little realization that one of the most difficult aspects of that effort is learning to tolerate one's self. When "Know Thyself" was the first of three maxims inscribed on the Temple of Apollo at Delphi, it was already old, and it has been echoed down the years by philosophers and poets. It involves facing the realities which so easily fill one with terror, and yet learning to find not only satisfaction, but joy, in living. Not all the aid of psychiatry or even of religious leadership can assure self-mastery. Those, and many other resources, may help, but the attainment of any measure of success is wholly individual; each must undertake the struggle for himself.

Such private life of the spirit is essential; a private life of the mind is also necessary. Turning to a book between appointments, bringing contrast into the day's activity by reading for recreation instead of for credit—this habit should be cultivated in college. Otherwise it is unlikely ever to be established at all. It can grow best where the student has a reasonable opportunity to be alone.

The fraternities have long been in need of physical, financial, social, and intellectual reform. Now all are confronted with a radical change in their entire way of life. The shift is so dramatic that it should make other kinds of change seem easy. I am an optimist, or I should long since have abandoned my profession. Yet I am not so steeped in roseate dreams that I think the undergraduate chapters can achieve a new life without help. They will have the active and sympathetic cooperation of the University officers; that will not be enough. Assistance from two other sources is required.

All the chapters belong to national fraternities; considerable sums of money flow from the local members to their national organizations. In return the chapters have a right and the University has a right to expect them to supply real leadership to their members. National offices should share in stimulating an intellectual interest. Once that was the cornerstone of fraternity life; too often now the stone which the builders set at the head of the corner has seemed rejected. The central organizations of some of the older fraternities with the greatest prestige have failed to supply adequate moral and intellectual leadership. For the fees there should be a *quid pro quo* much more significant than has been available for many years.

The alumni are the second source of help. It is not enough to come back and relive youth's purple passages by recounting to cynical younger brothers the wayward exploits of salad days. Each generation is sufficiently ingenious to contrive its own devilment without the stimulation of alumni in their "anecdotage." Moreover, tradition, which casts a golden haze over even shoddy practices, will supply any deficiencies in the students' already active imaginations. From the alumni the undergraduates need manifestations of maturity of interest, judgment, and temper. They need assistance in bridging the inevitable gap between youth and the elders who bear the daily responsibility of college government. Many an alumnus whose financial status will not permit him to enrich the University can add to its intellectual and moral endowment by exerting influence which he is in a singularly strategic position to exercise. There have been notable instances of such leadership; the times urgently call for more.

Within the memory of many here 85 per cent or more of the students belonged to fraternities; virtually every boy who wanted to join had such an opportunity. Today fewer than half the students are members. Many causes have contributed to this change. These new houses will help correct several of them. One phase of the reform, however, lies with the chapters themselves. Fraternities must justify their position, not on the basis of exclusiveness, but through their capacity for fellowship. Snobbery cannot be excused on the ground that it is a private vice; it runs too deeply counter to the democratic ideal; it is too fundamentally hostile to democratic practice. Every trace of it should be rooted out of our campus.

By deliberate design the student body is drawn from a wide geographical range, from the whole economic spectrum, from some newly come to this country and from others whose lineage reaches back to our earliest times. The liberal college is predicated upon a society fluid in structure where every individual meets opportunity without barriers of race, religion, or economic or social status. Brown fraternities should be constructive forces in the progress toward appreciating people for their minds and characters and personalities, and for nothing else.

I have suggested some means for the realization of a distinctive way of life among all the students at Brown. Those goals are no easier of attainment than these buildings proved to be. Before us, however, is the substance of things hoped for. Now there is opportunity, unparalleled in the history of Brown University, to exploit these physical instrumentalities for social, cultural, moral, and intellectual gains.

VIII ✒ President Wayland's 1850
Report to the Corporation

IT IS one hundred years since the famous "Report to the Corporation," written by President Francis Wayland after long reflection upon observations made while on leave of absence studying institutions of learning in Great Britain and France. Some of his recommendations are as pertinent now as they were in 1850. Foremost among them, of course, is the proposal to house students intelligently and in a way which might assist the University to fulfill its educational function by making residences aids instead of obstacles to learning.

There was occasion to comment upon this aspect of Wayland's report when we were considering the housing problem nearly ten years ago. Since that time the trend among universities and colleges has been strongly away from his proposals and toward the sort of buildings he deprecated. He denounced student living quarters that seemed more like barracks than homes.

Thirty years ago it looked as though his advice was to be followed. The construction of the Harvard Houses, the Yale Colleges, and the quadrangles at the University of Chicago typified what was happening all across the

Excerpt from the President's Report to the Corporation, June 3, 1950

country in institutions both public and private. An effort was made to give the student at least the opportunity for quiet, books close at hand, adult leadership, and a civilized style in dining. In institutions designed not only to promote learning but to improve manners, in schools intended to stimulate appreciation as well as expand knowledge, all this was heartening.

But in the period since the war that humanistic trend has been sharply reversed. New buildings have cut to the absolute minimum the cubic space available to students; they have been constructed in long rows upon a kind of production line basis. Little or no attention has been paid to evoking quiet—indeed, they are the noisiest structures ever used for students to live in. Furniture is conspicuously institutional and, in at least one instance, not only is no provision made for supplying pictures or for hanging them on the walls, the use of pictures is specifically prohibited. It is hard to see how the attainment of an anti-civilizing environment can go much further.

Service in dining rooms has all but disappeared, and the practice of placing steam tables in the middle of oak-paneled dining halls, with nothing but cafeteria service, and of having students eat from wartime trays instead of dishes has become common. Practically none of the new dining halls is planned for any other type of service. Moreover, their capacity is calculated to a nicety; the goal of every study is how to expedite the chow line whereas a quarter of a century ago emphasis was upon leisure, quiet, and good conversation in the dining hall.

It is appropriate to invite attention to these developments and to emphasize again that in our housing program we are trying to abide by Wayland's admonition; Andrews Hall and the Quadrangle run counter to these newer trends. The Refectory is designed for table service, with all the students seated at one time instead of eating in shifts; the room is arranged so that table conversation is possible. As for the fraternity houses and dormitories, modern construction has been modified enough to insure quiet—so far as that is feasible with boys. The buildings will lack some of the refinements which make Andrews Hall one of the quietest dormitories in the country because, since its construction, costs have advanced to such a degree as to put them out of reach. Against all current trends lounge space has been provided.

Another of President Wayland's ideas, expressed in his famous report, has had a somewhat similar fate. The democratic passion he expressed has become so common, at least in form, that its originality and historic significance are overlaid. Unhappily Wayland's desire for education to "look with as kindly an eye on the mechanic as the lawyer, on the manufacturer and merchant as the minister," while it has come to pass, has been realized at a level far below that which he had in mind.

He did not place the emphasis upon training or vocationalism as such; he was interested in raising "to high intellectual culture the whole mass of our people"; he wanted the artisan, the merchant, and the manufacturer each to perform "his process with a knowledge of the laws by which it is governed," to be transformed "from an unthinking laborer into a practical philosopher." Moreover, Christianity was to "imbue the whole mass of our people with the spirit of universal love." This accent upon culture, upon basic laws, and upon the spirit of love shows that he was not concerned with the techniques, with the routine skills which modern vocationalism has so thoroughly emphasized; his emphasis was upon value judgments, intellectual discipline, and moral perception which have virtually disappeared from modern vocationalism.

His idea, many would say, has been accepted; in reality it has been debased. There is nothing wrong with training as such; what is wrong is that training alone is inadequate. Volumes are being written upon the subject— and verbally there is relatively little disagreement. There is endless insistence upon training for citizenship, for social betterment; but the programs for those objectives are inadequate because of the obsession with training in its narrower meaning. In this field, as in housing, the fundamental idea of Wayland is valid, but its attainment requires the reversal of present trends.

Some other reforms Wayland proposed have become general, but have run so far beyond the scope of his intention as to defeat his purpose. The free elective system is one such. He wanted to let each student "study what he chose, all that he chose, and nothing but what he chose" in college. Reading that language outside its historical context gives the impression that what he wished has come to pass—disastrously. If one looks more carefully at the scope of action he proposed and sought to carry into effect, a wholly different impression is gained.

Furthermore, Wayland argued that the world was not enough with us, that universities had lost touch with the work-a-day task and needed to get closer to current problems and concern themselves more actively with them. He could not have foreseen that a hundred years later the great problem would be to disentangle university teaching from day-to-day events so that students could attain perspective and depth of knowledge from the reservoir of past experience which history supplies, so that they could achieve a structure of values which grows from philosophy and religion, and could appreciate the theoretical foundation which is available in economics and the sciences. All these are necessary if men are to deal with something more than symptoms and make a real contribution to the resolution of problems that press upon us.

History consists of both change and continuity. Thinking back over the century since the Report, which was so outstanding that it gained nation-wide attention and stamped Brown for a considerable period as a leading progressive and alert institution, we can see that any sense of newness today is more superficial than valid, that the basic factors—life within the University, great teaching, and eager learning—continue to be our goals.

IX ✐ Dedication of Andrews Hall

Today we join in tribute to all who participated in making the new dormitory possible. Their names are legion. To each one I express the gratitude of Brown University, and particularly of Pembroke College in Brown University.

There is a philosophy of history which assumes that the pressures of society create events, that individuals are merely the instruments of social forces which determine their actions. There is a contrary theory that men create the conditions under which they function and that biography is therefore the key to history. Most people find that a synthesis which encompasses both is more reasonable than a mere choice between two extreme positions. Hitler could never have achieved dominance had not the social, economic, and political situation opened the door for his tactics. In normal times his extravagances would not have influenced more than a lunatic fringe. However, there is no indication in the experience of the world that, if the circumstances had been different, Hitler would have been an admirable character. It takes both the man and the occasion to achieve a given result—good or bad.

The founding of Pembroke College illustrates the

Pembroke College, November 2, 1947

validity of this synthesis. Today we dedicate a building and give it the name of a man. We have chosen the name because we think of E. Benjamin Andrews as the founder of Pembroke. But even so great a man as he could not have founded the college alone. Before he became President of Brown University, the social pressures to which he responded had already been felt. The Corporation had considered the matter sympathetically; the faculty had made suggestions as to how to achieve the objective. President Robinson had approved the idea in principle, and had seen only practical difficulties as a barrier; except for his age, he would have been willing to undertake the project. He knew that it would take vigor, imagination, and courage even to "cooperate with the inevitable."

It is difficult after half a century to see what made the decision so hard. As one reads the arguments against the proposal to admit women they seem unreal. There was, for example, the legal and literal idea that the word "youth" in our Charter referred to men only and that the admission of women might void the Charter; dictionaries and literature were searched to justify or overthrow that contention. There were deliberations about the propriety of using certain classrooms; in retrospect these discussions seem to have magnified small obstacles. There were questions of finance which daunted some of the most courageous, but which as time went on solved themselves.

Perhaps we can draw one lesson from this perspective upon the founding of Pembroke. Sooner or later women will be elected to the Corporation of Brown University. There is no question of their ability, or their interest—or of their financial resources. In a day when so much is said against discrimination, the exclusion of women is surely an anachronism. Our successors 50 years hence will be amazed at the hesitation and the doubts which have so far precluded their election.

I am reminded that the appointment of women to the faculty and their assignment to teach men as well as women happened so gradually, so naturally, that it passed unnoticed even by those who made the change. The progress by which the very limited offerings to Pembroke students were expanded until all undergraduate courses are open to them provides another illustration of the way in which barriers fall with time. It would be difficult to identify any single act, or any particular moment, when the last obstacle to free access disappeared.

In a crisis Horace Greeley once gave some sound advice. The United States had suspended the payment of gold to its citizens during the Civil War. How to resume specie payments was discussed with much learning and at even greater length—with some light and even more heat. Horace Greeley brought the whole discussion down to earth; said he, "The way to resume is to resume." One day, without fanfare, his advice was taken and it was found that the resumption of gold payment presented no problem whatever. The fiscal situation had matured to a point where it required only the courage to perform the act. Horace Greeley may have shown the way to elect women to the Corporation.*

Even before President Andrews assumed office many people were willing to have women admitted to Brown University. What was the distinctive contribution that would solve the problem? It was the readiness to take the chances inherent in any new project. There were social

*In 1949 Anna Canada Swain '11 was elected a member of the Board of Trustees of Brown University. The late Virginia Piggott Verney '28 became the second woman Trustee in 1951. Other alumnæ have subsequently been elected to the Board.

chances, for the segregation of the sexes in New England colleges was a fetish at the time; it was feared that the prestige of the institution might suffer by running counter to the current. There were financial chances, for the women's college might not draw support adequate to justify the outlay. There was a chance, too, that the education of women might take a tack so radically different from that of men that there would be no economy or efficiency in having a women's college in what had been a men's university.

Recently we hear a good deal about "calculated risk." It is the opposite of a gambler's risk, where everything is hazarded upon events wholly out of control of the person who takes the chance. A calculated risk is the kind a reasonable man accepts after considering the entire situation. He retains some, though by no means complete, control over the consequences. The founder of Pembroke was no gambler, but he knew the meaning of risk and freely accepted the hazards.

Thus the occasion was ripe and the man was ready. By inheritance, by taste, by training, and by experience E. Benjamin Andrews was passionately interested in education. His idea of education was a union, indeed a fusion, of intellectual and moral elements. He saw no point in knowledge without purpose and no reason to train the mind unless its impulses were controlled by moral principles.

He was a man of vast energy and force of character. In his youth he suffered the handicaps of poverty; in our day he would be regarded as one of the underprivileged; it would be said that with his resources he could not hope to go to college. He was injured as a child, so that he had to be out of school for long periods. His preparatory work was interrupted by service in the Civil War, which cost him an eye, so that he might have been considered permanently handicapped. However, he transformed the losses of the underprivileged into profits. In the fight to get ahead he developed a zest for life which made all experience a great adventure. He learned to earn his living—meager from some points of view, but rich from others—without fear. Self-reliance carried him serenely through severe trials; he surmounted privations without a trace of self-pity. In short, the disciplines of adversity made him a man whom nothing could daunt. When hardship, or ill health, or defeat blocked the road, he mustered what patience he could until he was able to resume the course of action upon which his mind was determined.

Andrews lacked a deep attachment to any particular region. If his father was not an itinerant minister, he was certainly peripatetic, and Benjamin had no permanent home. He had no single preparatory school; he went to three. He had one college and one theological school, but between college and theological school he taught and was principal of an academy; after his schooling in divinity he had a brief pastorate. Only six years out of college, at the age of 31, he became a college president and spent four years as the dynamic leader of Denison University. There followed three years as professor in Newton Theological Seminary, then five years as professor at Brown, one as professor at Cornell, nine years as President of Brown, two as Superintendent of Schools in Chicago, and then eight as Chancellor of the University of Nebraska.

If his background and youthful experience gave him no strong geographical attachments, the roots of his personality grew deeply into an intellectual and moral ideal. He fully exemplified the familiar scriptural passage, "The zeal of thine house hath eaten me up." He pursued his ideal wherever the best opportunity for effectiveness appeared at any given moment. So deep was this devotion that it seemed inflexible. Superficially it might make him appear to have lacked institutional loyalty. Such a conclusion would be wide of the mark. He knew the survival power of institutions to be greater than the lives of individuals; he never over-estimated the essentiality of his own contribution to a particular situation. Moreover, he perceived that sometimes a man can render the greatest service to an institution by forcing it to face a vital issue, even if it involved his own displacement.

It cannot be said that President Andrews succeeded in everything he undertook. Like Wayland before him he reshaped the intellectual and moral life so vigorously, he reformed educational practices so zealously, he concentrated upon student progress so whole-heartedly that he did not find money in quantities sufficient to endow adequately what his love and labor achieved. His successes were the kind essential to lively educational progress; he knew that quality of work would ultimately draw support. But for Andrews, as for Wayland, it came too slowly.

E. Benjamin Andrews made mistakes, but he was the first to proffer candid acknowledgment when he received more light. Concerning his position on the issue of the free coinage of silver in a ratio of sixteen to one with gold, which occasioned the difficulty at Brown, he said five years later, "I have to admit that it was an astounding mistake and that I was in great and inexcusable error." That was a remarkable expression; it reflected the sincerity which was the key to his character. He could have changed his mind and remained silent, taking advantage of the fact that he was then half a continent away. He could have said the circumstances had altered, as indeed they appeared to have. He could have weaseled his expression; but he scorned to soften his own responsibility. Such was his character that he would never be as severe with anyone else as with himself.

Inflexibility in pursuit of an ideal did not in the slightest degree reduce his personal charm, his geniality, his lively, comprehensive interest in every phase of student life. No professor, no president was ever more dearly loved; none inspired deeper or more permanent respect and affection. All knew that he was without personal ambition and devoted to the welfare of those committed to his charge. He evoked hero worship from a multitude of students—and never let it go to his head. He never played for their approval, and was never inflated by it.

How he remained solvent is a mystery; he was forever loaning money, much of it never repaid. He understood, sympathized with—and officially suppressed—student ebullience. He shared it fully until it went too far; but he set the metes and bounds with a hand so firm and a skill so sure that his decision was beyond challenge. For personal problems, or difficulties of whatever kind, he had a ready and sympathetic ear, a sensible and strong suggestion. Without losing anything of the dignity that then hedged his office, he exhibited an informality which has left memories replete with anecdote.

Andrews was a teacher. He knew all the arts—not just some of them. He was an ardent and omnivorous reader. He amassed great quantities of information, and reflected upon it, reducing it to order, searching out meanings. Lucid in exposition, eloquent in expression, original in illustration, racy in the use of words, resourceful in the construction of phrases, he inspired, he led, he stimulated, he amused, and he irritated. In short, he took whatever course was necessary to produce an intellectual response. The profound sincerity that characterized his instruction led to appreciation even when it did not bring agreement or conviction.

Andrews was a professor at Brown for only five years, and while he held the office of president for nine, he was on leave of absence one whole year and part of another, so he was actually in residence not more than seven and a half years. Yet no one holding a responsible post in this University, even 50 years later, can help realizing that his administration was a turning point. Under Andrews Brown ceased to be a small New England college and embraced the idea of a university. With him the ideal of scholarship, which must dominate a modern university, came to fruition. Graduate work was put upon a solid basis. The thorny problem of the accommodation of women was solved in a manner both statesmanlike and tactful. The principles of academic freedom were dramatized and justified not only for Brown, but for all universities and colleges. It took unique strength so to infuse this institution with so many ideas in so short a time as to set it upon a course from which it has never deviated.

As for Pembroke, his conviction and his courage were so profound that for the first few years he carried personally the financial responsibility for the venture. In retrospect the hazards do not appear overwhelming, but in prospect they would have daunted a less doughty warrior. Pembroke Hall was constructed during the year when he was on leave from the University because of overwork and exhaustion; it was dedicated 50 years ago this month. Its completion brought to attainment one of his principal objectives. Until then the Women's College had been "an adjunct." That did not satisfy him. As he expressed it, "no mere 'annex' is desired or intended. The College must be part and parcel of the University, giving women students the full university status." With the dedication of Pembroke Hall his goal was fully achieved.

Is it any wonder the largest building on the Pembroke campus is now named Andrews Hall?

X ↙ Fifty Years—
Success or Failure?

W E MEET today in an atmosphere of triumph and hope. Fifty years ago, under the pressure of some bold women and with the leadership of a vigorous man, the hesitant Corporation of Brown University took what now appears to have been a halting and timid step. Because the women did not lose their boldness and the men found their powers of resistance steadily eroded, as is the case in all well-regulated families, Pembroke College became a success. Today the prospects for its future are not only infinitely brighter than they were in 1891, but brighter than they have ever been. The troubles from which Pembroke now suffers are incident to growth and maturity; they are not the pioneer struggles involved in getting started. Without the minor troubles of prosperity the sense of adventure might be lost. We might slack off and fail to exploit fully our great opportunities.

. . . . . .

America has certainly led in the democratization of education. If one were to search for a modern illustration

Excerpt. Opening Convocation, Pembroke's Semi-Centennial Year, September 24, 1941

of the classless society, he would find it more perfectly exemplified in the educational world than anywhere else. Teachers are drawn from every economic level, every social background. Students in like manner represent extraordinary differentiation in respect to ability and economic resources and cultural heritage. They are diverse in every way in which human beings can be diverse, for the classless society is in no way hostile to the idea of individualism; indeed it is utterly dependent upon individualism.

Our American colleges constitute a society within which a person of vision and energy, industry and character can make of himself what he wishes. They are places where one finds no privilege, no right that is not bound up with an equivalent duty or responsibility. It is the essence of education that there is no privilege which money can buy. There is no privilege which birth can achieve. There is no attainment which a student can demand as his own right without having to win it. Participation in extra-curricular activities, honors awards, Phi Beta Kappa all depend upon ability and hard work. Rewards are not conditioned by anything but achievement, save in the rare instances where abuses have prostituted the normal functioning of the educational process. Even then the student can have only the husk of the reward without its substance.

Another of the great triumphs of education is the advance in the quality, as well as in the range and inclusiveness, of its work. Two opposing factions here meet on common ground. One group which regards itself as the exponent of reform insists that standards have been kept so high that they discourage students. When one reads the publications of these advocates of reform, so-called, the really terrifying thing is not the indictment they make of

the educational process; it is the revelation of their lack of
faith in the dignity, industry, and capacity of our youth.
God help youth if they fall into the hands of leaders who
pity instead of respect them. Men and women who teach
grow to a realization that our greatest failure is in under-
estimating the intelligence and character of students. It is
not reform to abuse them by needless pity.

On the other hand, at the opposite extreme these self-
styled reformers are met on common ground by academic
hardshells who cry that standards have been lowered. The
use of the word "standards" itself is unfortunate. It is
borrowed from industrial practice and intimates measures
which are definite and rigid, though no such measures
exist or can exist in an enterprise like education. It predicates something absolute which is correct; everything
else falls short. In human achievement that is a false, and
even pernicious, assumption. It totally overlooks the nature of man and the historical realities of our experience.

It is well known that not only do larger numbers, but
a very much larger percentage of our youth go on to institutions of higher education. It is equally obvious that
the quality of scholarship has advanced in many respects
in the last century. We have overcome many weaknesses.
This is transparent when one remembers the criticism of
education one hundred years ago, its overdependence on
memory and lack of emphasis on originality and creative
work. Those were gross shortcomings.

Many of the colleges of one hundred years ago would
not be regarded as the equal of a modern high school. In
the preparation of teachers, both in their knowledge of
their fields of instruction and in their professional capacity, there has been an enormous advance. The talk
of lowered standards, therefore, stems from a false and

deceptive terminology, from lack of historical perspective, from current pessimism about the present and alarm about the future, rather than from any just estimate of the actual situation.

This is by no means to assert that the current status is beyond criticism or that it represents the ultimate in achievement. I recall these facts only to drive home the point that we can improve our work by setting our goals still further ahead, by approaching them positively rather than by depreciating the substantial achievements of the recent past.

There is another criticism of American education which seems to me to misstate the problem. It is one of the clichés of current discussion that American education lacks unity, that it is chaotic, that no two institutions have like aims or objectives—or "end products," which is an extraordinary name for an alumna. Yet when one stops to think of it, that is not a weakness at all. On the contrary, it would be a fairer criticism to say that American education has borrowed the concept of standard interchangeable parts from industry in too great a degree. Units, credits, hours, and all the mechanistic jargon of academic interchangeable parts have fastened a leech-like hold upon us, so that individualistic non-conformists in these matters are looked upon with suspicion. When an institution—such as Brown, for example—breaks away from this terminology, it is called upon to supply a key which will translate its expressions into the language it has deliberately abandoned.

But if we turn from terms to substance, variety represents strength, not weakness. I would lay emphasis upon this aspect of our experience which I regard as one of the great triumphs in education—namely, the profound differences which lie beneath the paper-thin surface of standardized interchangeable terms. They are standardized only in form; they are interchangeable only in recorders' offices; they represent no substantial reality whatever. The reality is individuality.

Therefore, we should take pride today in the fact that Pembroke is not like any other women's college, that it has unique qualities. They are not the product of self-conscious efforts to be different. Pembroke was not designed to be unique; it grew that way. That is all to the good, for in the best sense of the term, all growth is unique. In our country it is peculiarly so. The extent of the United States is so vast, the conditions of life arising from geographical factors such as climate, soil, and so forth are so various, racial stocks are so different, and conditions so contrasting that inevitably there are enormous and healthy variations in the tone of voice, in the accent of speech, in the rhythm of life—and consequently in the educational process of the individual.

This variety has been stimulated and made greater by the local control of education. The federal government does relatively little in the field and state governments only a moderate amount, the principal initiative being left to local communities and private philanthropy. When men fasten their eyes upon smaller foreign nations with more centralized governments and a different philosophy of life, the variety observed in American education is misinterpreted as confusion, or even chaos. It is neither confusion nor chaos. It is the manifestation of the vitality of individuality in the midst of a world that happens for a moment to be bemused by goose-stepping under Boards of Regents and other standardizing agencies.

I do not know what the next 50 years will bring to

Pembroke. In the very best sense of the phrase, I do not care—taking no anxious thought for the morrow. I believe that the dynamic of its life will carry it forward. I would not want to engage in that modern pastime of making a plan for the next 50 years, for I would not want to shackle the growth of Pembroke to the measure of my faith, great as that faith may be. Much less would I tether it to the measure of my courage or my imagination. Let us do our work well today and trust those who follow. The Pembroke of today is not the Pembroke of the plans or hopes or even the dreams of 50 years ago. It is something vastly better; it is not only larger, it is more vigorous and more fully unique.

What seems to me most important is that, in a time which laments its confusion, we should keep our minds upon the basic ideas and principles which remain outside the area of confusion. We should not allow ourselves to be disconcerted. Faith, courage, and energy will pay dividends over the next 50 years as they have in the half century that is gone.

XI ⚭ Spiritual Hospitality

"Covet earnestly the best gifts: and yet shew I unto you a more excellent way."   (I Corinthians XII: 31)

COLLEGE, if it is to have any social justification or any individual value, is a strenuous experience. Neither the economic life of the world nor the political state of the world nor current social philosophy nor ethical considerations leave room for an aristocracy or a leisure class.

With so much hunger and want and misery in the world, there is no justification for carrying non-economic activities up to the age of 21 or 22 and beyond unless there is a deferred social dividend which warrants the investment of time, money, and energy. That is why all the jokes about the campus as a country club, once so common, carried with them bitter overtones.

Fortunately, we have not heard so many of them in recent years. The aftermath of the second World War was almost precisely the opposite from that of the first World War. Veterans came back in a more serious mood; they were more determined, more intellectually industrious. The colleges have sought to capitalize on that momentum and to maintain a vigorous and active life.

I would not have it otherwise. College, if it is to be

Brown University Vespers, September 27, 1953

worth while, is hard work, and unless it is hard work it is an evil thing.

Nonetheless, the ancient saw that "all work and no play makes Jack a dull boy" has a modern equivalent. It is not only play that Jack needs to avoid being a dull boy; he needs another type of experience to keep him from being insensitive. It has to do with leisure, for even the most strenuous career requires some time for a wholly different rhythm of activity.

It is of that contrasting type of action which cannot be neglected without impoverishment that I would speak. Its cultivation necessitates the development of habits appropriate to its particular character.

Perhaps I can best explain it in terms of a spring. In a lovely spot on the shores of Lake Michigan, by a combination of knowledge, skill, and intuitive insight, a friend of mine found a hidden spring. He cleared out the debris and cut away the soil so that fresh, living water came bubbling up through the sand. It was sparkling, pure, and refreshing, of a constant temperature winter and summer. It seemed like a perpetual joy. But one winter when the storms were unusually severe and gales had thrust an ice-flow up the bank, the whole contour of the shore was changed and I could find no sign whatever of the living water. Only when the man who had originally discovered it came back was it possible to locate and restore the spring.

In much the same way as storms hid the living water, so over-intense activities tend to conceal and make unavailable well-springs which refresh life. My suggestion today is that you should seek out such well-springs. You will then use and enjoy their sparkling and refreshing quality. Without care of this kind the spiritual life, the aesthetic life, and many other facets of life are so effectively overlaid with the litter of daily routines—both of labor and of pleasures—as to be completely hidden and even forgotten.

A fruitful life of the mind, social experience, and physical enjoyment are among the best things to be "coveted." Nonetheless there is a "more excellent way." It is to find for yourself some new appreciation of beauty, some fresh fountain of thought, some clearer and finer aesthetic feeling, some deeper and truer spiritual experience. You will then attain a hitherto unrealized richness, as my friend found upon the property he had bought something way beyond his expectations.

How is it to be done? For my text requires that you be "shewn" the "more excellent way." Let us begin by saying that it cannot be done in any go-getter style. The urge to mastery is irrelevant. Instead it calls for an attitude of mental and spiritual hospitality—quiet reflection upon familiar guests who visit your mind and spirit.

I remember a letter received many years ago from an artist who exercised a very large influence upon a wide circle of friends in the course of a long life. She was staying at her summer home; in the midst of the letter she wrote this sentence: "I chewed a little while, gazing out into the greenest of orchards, with its flitting and singing birds." She was saying in her own way what Wordsworth wrote many years before:

> One impulse from a vernal wood
> May teach you more of man,
> Of moral evil and of good,
> Than all the sages can.
>
> .   .   .   .
>
> Enough of Science and of Art;
> Close up those barren leaves;
> Come forth, and bring with you a heart
> That watches and receives.

It was "a heart that watched and received" which was the key to one whole phase of a useful as well as a happy and a successful life. It would have been impossible to attain those objectives only by chewing "a little while, gazing out into the greenest of orchards, with its flitting and singing birds." On the other hand, if life had consisted of love and labor without this time of quiet hospitality to impression, much of its vividness, its depth, and its charm would have been lost.

Let us take art as an illustration. I do not deprecate the *study* of art; on the contrary, we should do everything to promote it. Yet one cannot see people searching for culture without awareness that for many the quest is self-defeating. This summer I saw a good deal of art in some of the castles, great homes, and museums of England. But as guides led the people through successive galleries, many could not be said to have "walked"—they trudged. In the slant of their shoulders and the ill-suppressed yawns they gave all the outward signs of museum fatigue.

Anyone who goes into the Louvre and tries to look at everything reminds me of nothing so much as a person who would enter a butcher shop, ask for an ounce of every kind of meat in the place, try to mix it all up in one meal, and then digest it. The mere description of that process is so fantastic as to reveal its folly. No one would think of doing such a thing. Every sensible person makes a selection based upon many factors such as taste, cost, individual preference; he chooses one at a time and varies his diet. It should be so with art, especially when one is seeking to be hospitable to its impressions, to know it and not merely to know about it.

The first necessity of relaxed hospitality is warm acquaintance. You cannot enjoy strangers as you do old friends. It is so with an object of art. I have seen many times, in the Metropolitan Museum in New York, a cup fashioned by Benvenuto Cellini over four hundred years ago. I have read Cellini's own account of his life; at one time I knew much about his position in history and particularly in the history of art. That cup is worthy of study, but there is another way to regard it—as a familiar object, as something which you have long possessed spiritually without holding property title to it. After you have become familiar with it, if you view only that cup and nothing else whatever, it fully repays a visit to the museum.

Or go to the Rembrandt room and to no other; after you are familiar with what is hung there, let one or two of the paintings absorb your attention. That is the idea which lies behind the rental collection of reproductions here at Brown. They are not merely for room decoration, though they help achieve that end; they are certainly not to instruct you, though they can have that effect. If the picture is worthy of being on your wall, it should become a familiar companion of your life; some part of each day contemplate it; regard it at various times and in various lights until every part of it lives in your imagination. If you do that, you may own the picture is a sense far more real than the man who possesses the original, particularly if he has many others and owns this one as an example of a certain artist's work, or because it was a good investment, or for any of the other thousand and one reasons for purchasing any kind of property.

If you have any talent whatever, draw or paint. That is now fashionable, since Winston Churchill and Dwight Eisenhower both find relaxation and enjoyment in it. But do not do it as a means of neural therapy, though it may well prove profitable in that regard. Do it to see for yourself what the artist means when he speaks of line, mass, form, and color. The quality of your pictorial result is not vital; if the reputation of Sir Winston and the President rested upon their painting, they would not be leaders in the world. The important thing is the refinement of your own appreciation; you may live with some great picture with a keener awareness of what makes it a significant element in your life. Thus you will establish a kinship with all artists and with all art. You will have found a spring of living water which will constantly refresh you.

Music can be approached in the same way. In my youth I never had an opportunity to study it; except for patriotic songs there was none in the public schools. There was, indeed, a glee club which sang "Songs by the fire, pass the pipe, pass the bowl," and other glees of similar quality. In the city where I lived there was no symphony orchestra, no artist series; victrola records were on wax and squawked; and the radio had not been developed. After college I did sit in the back seat of the new Boston Opera House and heard Mary Garden and Bassano and other great artists of that era singing their famous roles. From a remote corner of Symphony Hall I heard the Boston Symphony Orchestra under the baton of Karl Muck. In those years there was an element of striving to fill a gap of which I had suddenly become aware.

But that is not the sort of need of which I am speaking. Fulfillment of the kind I have in mind began when I was given a recording of the "Nutcracker Suite" by Tchaikovsky. It seemed to me weird and quite meaningless upon first hearing, but after I had played it again and again and listened to some part of it for a time every day, not while doing something else, but with body relaxed and mind composed and every tension released, all the threads in the web of melody became familiar, the pattern revealed itself with clarity and distinctness.

If you will do that with any good piece of music, every theme and every variation upon it can become completely your own. Speculate upon the forms and subtleties of form, upon the imagery which the music suggests and which may have suggested it to the composer. It is in these moments of quiet reflection (not upon strange things but upon familiar things) that you gain insights which are quite new; then all music will mean more to you. You will have achieved an advance in taste which will be a permanent element in your life; you will have found an undiscovered, a hidden, spring, a source of ever-flowing enjoyment and richness.

Or take books. Books are of many sorts and kinds and for many purposes. In college they are for the most part tools for the acquisition of knowledge and you should learn to use them effectively to that end. Other books are for sheer recreation, to divert the mind when it is over-serious, to amuse it when it is tired, to take you out of yourself for a time. But the best books have a great contribution of a different kind to make to your life.

They may be the same books that at one phase of your life you labor over; at another time you reflect upon them. In college I took "Six Plays of Shakespeare," studying them intensively. I memorized many of the principal speeches; we were required to give the act and scene and circumstances of any quotation for which the professor asked. There was little thrill in such study, but it was an essential groundwork. Ever since, when I reread one of those plays, the familiarity gained with such arduous effort is distilled into appreciation. I could no longer pass the examination, but there is new depth of enjoyment; the

majesty, the humor, the dignity of life and its tragic in-
sufficiency are all made explicit. There is a world of philosophy and wisdom. One is caught up in the spirit of the
drama; the characters take on reality and play their roles
with genuine intensity.

It makes no difference what you read if it be worthy
and if it makes a contribution to your life. Poetry has its
own special appeal. If you submit to its mood in a time
of relaxation, it can speak to you in accents different from
any other, for when a thought is clothed in emotion and
stated with beauty, you are carried out of yourself into the
mind and heart of the poet.

In this mood you should read books not for the story
alone, not at a rapid pace, but following the rhythm of
the prose or the poetry, accepting the beauty of the words
as images, seeing scenery that you have never seen,
coming to know as real people those whom the author has
created. Read in reflective quiet; do not hesitate to stop
and wander with your own thoughts when your mind is
stirred. You may be weeks reading one book; it is almost
certain to be one you have read before, perhaps many
times; familiarity brings depth. If you learn to love books
and find in them a life apart from the day's task, you need
never again be captive to your labors. You may choose
your own way of life in moments of leisure and find books
to fit it.

Or take an illustration from nature. Some men, as they
go to their offices, might as well be blindfolded and
whisked there by magic. Their faces are set, their eyes on
the sidewalk, their minds already at the desk. The tension
involved in their business has already claimed them. Some
students walk this campus like automatons; they have
eyes but see not; ears have they but they hear not. There

is another way to cross the campus: it is with full awareness, seeing the texture and color of the buildings, the variety and characteristics of the trees, the patterns of the walks. The birds are not so numerous here as in some places, but nonetheless there are many; you can admire their grace, delicacy, and color. Accept as you walk the streets, wherever you are, whatever there is of beauty—of tree or flower or cloud or hill. Then all beauty will mean more to you.

Do all these things with music, and art, and literature, and nature, but not in any possessive spirit. Do not be so egocentric as that would imply. Rather let truth and beauty possess you. Modern physics tells us about the interpenetrability of matter, but like most scientific discovery the poet was there before the scientist:

> *Ah, happy hills! ah, pleasing shade!*
> *Ah, fields beloved in vain!*
> *Where once my careless childhood stray'd,*
> *A stranger yet to pain:*
> *I feel the gales that from ye blow*
> *A momentary bliss bestow.*

The gales can blow into and through you, becoming part of your life.

Awareness may be either one of two kinds. It may come from a tight and tense surface of attention, something like a drum, where the slightest impact makes its rumbling echo. That is an impact from without, and the response is only an echo. But it may come, and much more richly and fully, by a species of relaxation and receptivity, which let beauty and meaning sink into you. The sunset can enter your spirit and awaken a response, and in so doing make you kin to all artists and poets.

You may be asking yourselves, "What has this to do

with religion?" I have been dealing with intangibles, in
music, art, and literature, where the deepest values are
emotional; where only the form is intellectual. But the
ultimate reality is of the spirit, where values are infinitely
more significant than the materials, where, though you
may own nothing tangible, you may yet possess these enriching treasures. Thus not "things," but life itself, becomes important. And when life becomes significant in
terms of spiritual values, the rubbish that conceals the
well-spring of religious life is cleared away, and naturally,
inevitably, you enter upon a religious experience.

In passing a news-stand I once saw an article by Harry
Emerson Fosdick entitled "After All Religion Is an Art."
The title is arresting, all by itself. It points to the fact that
only the form of religion and its expression are intellectual—that is, embodied in "theology." Its truth, its beauty,
the fresh waters of life run deeply through the emotions;
they can make us brothers to all prophets and mystics, as
music and art make us kin to composers and painters.

Then as we read the Scriptures we understand them
anew. "I will lift up mine eyes unto the hills, from
whence cometh my help." "The heavens declare the glory
of God; and the firmament sheweth his handiwork." "Ho,
everyone that thirsteth, come ye to the waters." These are
the expressions of men who have made the kind of approach to the religious life of which I have been speaking.

There are appropriate times to "fight the good fight
with all thy might"; there are times to "work for the night
is coming"; but there are also times to surrender to the
teachings of art, music, nature—and religion. As Wordsworth put it, "we can feed this mind of ours in a wise
passiveness."

Cultivate, then, in moments of leisure, snatched from

engrossing routine, a zestful receptivity, where all sound and color and form and imagery come to have a natural part in your life. Then all the wisdom, all the spiritual enrichment inherent in beauty, in imagination, and in action may be distilled by reflection into a religious faith which correlates and interprets the whole of life's experience.

XII ✒ Charles Evans Hughes

A S COLLEGE students you are likely to look upon
yourselves as subjects; I should prefer that you
regard yourselves as predicates. You tend to feel you are
subjects in two senses: first, subject to rules and discipline,
and to curricula; second, as people without sovereignty or
power of command, with no capacity to determine what
kind of college this is to be, what its qualities, its reputation, its function, and its product. It is usual to think of
yourselves as the governed, as being kept in leading-
strings at a time when you have reached a maturity of
which you are more conscious than the faculty appear
to be.

Today let us shift the emphasis from the subject to the
predicate—the action part of the sentence. Upon what
you do is predicated what sort of place this will be. If all
our buildings were marble halls, and all our sod creeping-
bent, thick and soft as velvet, if all our trees were hoary
elms weaving their shadow patterns upon storied walls;
and if we had a faculty unique in knowledge, sartorial elegance, and personal charm; and yet had poor students,
the institution would not attain a great or solid reputation
—and you would not get a good education.

Opening Convocation, Brown University, September 29, 1948

Some of you already know that not all our buildings are marble halls; you will discover in due course that not all the professors wear Arrow collars, at least they do not always achieve the pictorial effect of the advertisements. All that is, for the moment, beyond your control. But within your own competence is the determination of the quality of the education you will acquire here.

To illustrate the point I would like to speak about the undergraduate days of a Brown student who lived a long life and a full one. His days were marked by achievement and fame, but crossed by failure and tragedy. He was as human a man as I ever knew, and yet as great.

Charles Evans Hughes entered Brown in September, 1878, as a transfer student from Madison University, which now appears on our football schedule as Colgate. Back of him was neither wealth nor influence. He came unheralded and unknown; as the son of a Baptist minister, his financial resources were meager in the extreme.

He did not come to college with a fixed purpose beyond college itself. It is now standard practice to say that in "the good old days" students had already determined upon careers as ministers, teachers, lawyers, or doctors, and that the liberal arts college was really a direct preparation for professional life. But a study of the curriculum available in 1878 shows that it was poorly adapted to direct vocational ends. Moreover, anyone who knows anything about those professions knows that they are so diverse in their demands that no single curriculum could meet the professional needs of all.

An important characteristic of this new student was that he was ready to take one step at a time. He lived from day to day, exemplifying the maxim he must have heard a thousand times in home and church, "Take therefore no thought for the morrow." It did not deeply concern him, so far as the record goes or as he later recounted his college experiences, that he had no vocational objective. He was going to college to get what it had to offer. Then he would do the next thing. He was willing to let time and experience show what the next step was to be. Today we can look at him as any normal undergraduate. He was not a pre-law student or pre-anything else—just a college boy taking life in his stride.

It was not until late in his senior year and at the suggestion of a classmate that he turned toward the law. Indeed it was just before Commencement, when, as class prophet, he was writing about the future of his classmates, that he was challenged to say what he would do—and followed the advice of a fellow student. That is only a dramatic example of a vital element in college life then and now. As Hughes, himself, expressed it, "we exerted a strong influence upon each other." With all the changes that time has brought since 1878 that central fact of college life remains unaltered. Student influence is often far more potent than faculty advice or any other professional "guidance."

When he came to Brown, the future statesman was only 16 years old, though he had already spent two years in another college. He was tall, and not well developed physically. President Faunce who was a Junior in 1878 described him as "long, lank, extremely slender." He was never of varsity caliber and could not make a team; but he was interested in athletics and managed the baseball team one season. He was a consistent rooter, and made trips long before the days when hitch-hiking facilitated travel. He followed the team even when the modest cost was a serious drain on his resources.

Outside athletics he was a participant in all student activities. He served, as did his son and grandson, on the editorial staff of the student newspaper. What he wrote has been, to some extent at least, identified. It shows him as conforming perfectly to the undergraduate type. He wrote satiric advice to the department of buildings and grounds—good advice, too, which was acted upon a mere 60 years later, to the benefit of us all. He wrote a history of faculty rules and regulations and offered suggestions for further change. The greatest reform he advocated—abolition of the grading system—has not yet been achieved. It may come in time.

He joined a fraternity and entered actively into its life —forensic and intellectual as well as social. In college— and until the day of his death—he was a good story-teller and could sharpen the point by his hearty and dramatic way of recounting any episode. "He had the reputation of being one of the best wits of the class, and was very quick at repartee."

He did not lead his class in scholarship, though his standing was high. He was never a grind in any sense of the word. He took honors and prizes only when it appealed to him to do so, not with the efficient purposefulness of the grade-getter. He was the kind of student a teacher likes best—one who does the work for what there is in it, not for the grade or any other reward.

What was it then that marked this student and made him notable in college long before he attained national and, ultimately, international fame?

Three things: the first was rigid self-discipline, a habit that followed him through all the years of his long life. I saw him often when he was Secretary of State. He was the most prompt, devoted, and conscientious Secretary that we have had in modern times. You could almost set your watch by the time of his arrival at the cold granite structure across Executive Avenue from the White House. When he left he almost always carried a bag full of papers for study at home. He never discussed an issue with a foreign diplomat without having mastered not only the précis prepared by his staff but the entire documentation. It required a prodigious effort and long hours; but he followed the routine without exhaustion, for there was no waste motion.

He was Chief Justice when I came to Brown and several times I stayed in his home in Washington when in that city on University business. During his periods of leisure he was entirely relaxed and full of good conversation, but when the appointed time came for him to be at his desk that moment found him at his work and fully absorbed in it. Such habits of self-discipline were only the continuation of methods he followed in college.

Most people find it harder to get themselves to work than they do to labor after they start. Many people develop so much internal friction that they work against themselves more than at the job. People think of self-discipline as cramping their style and limiting happiness. Actually self-discipline is no kill-joy; when well developed it gives a relaxed sense of power and focuses the mind on the instant problem.

Concentration, it is called; but that is a poor word to describe efficient mental work. For when people concentrate consciously they are often thinking more about thinking than about the matter in hand. A better way of describing the characteristic of a disciplined mind is the absence of diffusion—complete escape from self-interruption, physical or mental, emotional or tangible.

For Charles Evans Hughes self-discipline had come, through long habit, no longer to require an effort of the will; on the contrary it released his will to effective constructive effort. When he read his college assignments he neither counted the pages nor measured the time, nor was aware of any other thing until the task was done. No one who wastes time has much leisure. The person who learns through consistent self-discipline to do his work is never too busy; he has leisure for other things.

Leisure suggests the second dominant characteristic of this student. He had time to spare and he used it for the best of all recreation—intellectual pleasure, emotional interest, broadening his taste, sharpening his perceptions. He read without guidance outside of class assignments— omnivorously. He read through most of Dickens while at Brown and told me of the immense enjoyment he had from it. If you have a lively and broad sense of humor, Dickens will delight you; if you have a deep social concern, Dickens will stimulate it; if you want to study human nature, Dickens is a rich mine. Hughes also read Thackeray, Macaulay, Victor Hugo, Emerson, Scott, Hawthorne, and many others. He read on many topics and always with zest. There was nothing of the prig in this wide reading, nothing of self-conscious self-improvement, no effort to learn "how to win friends and influence people." His reading was complete enjoyment of leisure time.

Hughes gained much in the classroom, but far beyond that he made direct acquaintance with the great literature of his day. Thus he acquired vicarious experience upon which he was able to draw throughout his life. He did not have to grope through every problem himself and learn every lesson at first hand; he could recall the issues and situations that historical and fictional characters had faced before and he knew the consequences of their choices.

There was a third characteristic of this youthful scholar which will make him seem almost as grim as the rigid self-discipline and the rich use of leisure time. He was not contemptuous of his memory. Recently it has been fashionable to admire "memory" from the grandstand. Many think dreamily how wonderful it would be to know all that John Kieran knows, but remain contemptuous of the process by which such omniscience in sports, poetry, natural history, and other fields is acquired. Some people have natural gifts of memory, but there is no aspect of the intellectual life which so repays cultivation.

The effort of memory is painful at first, but if the effort is long pursued it can produce a memory so muscular that remembering is as easy as breathing. When I was a very young historian a young mathematician made sport of me because I had to memorize so many dates. He said he would never adopt a vocation which drew so heavily upon the powers of memory. Whereupon he became a stock-broker and has had to recall from day to day, month to month, and year to year the quotations of many stocks, the highs and lows, the yield, the histories of numerous companies, the nature of their management—a welter of data which makes the memory task of the historian seem relatively simple by comparison.

What Charles Evans Hughes studied he remembered, what he read for pleasure in his leisure moments he was able to recall without effort. Over the years he cultivated that faculty. On one occasion when he was in private practice, during the interim between his two periods of service on the Supreme Court, I heard him argue before that body. His opponent—a former Attorney General of the United States—had copious notes and many assistants. Mr. Hughes spoke without a paper before him; quoted at length; gave citations by case, volume, and page. He did it unerringly, without strain or obvious effort.

Soon after I came to Brown he spoke at the Washington Alumni Dinner in March and agreed to give the same speech at Commencement in June. At that time he spoke from this platform and with no manuscript repeated the speech word for word. In the midst of one of the most exacting, time-consuming, and exhausting jobs in the United States it seemed as nothing for him to commit to memory an address that took half an hour to deliver.

While Hughes was at Brown he had great teachers. He said of them, "I could ask no greater privilege for any college student than to come under the direct guidance and inspiration of such men." President Robinson he called "majestic and severe"—"the embodiment of the moral law"—and as a disciplinarian, "terrifying." "If I learned to know the president well, I had the fear he knew me better." But as a teacher, who despised cant and hated sham, Robinson "shook youth out of carelessness and indifference into a realization of individual responsibility and power; the student went forth from his instruction with a new birth of purpose and courage."

John Lewis Diman, Professor of History and Political Economy, "stimulated [his students] to the highest pitch of effort and heroic endeavors in individual research." John Larkin Lincoln's liveliness of spirit and personal charm made him in the deepest sense of the word a teacher of the humanities. Albert Harkness, whose *Latin Grammar* was a work of art, will always be remembered as a teacher whose precise and exact scholarship, whose insistence upon the disciplines of precision, whose sense of proportion, and whose grace and finish of style made him outstanding.

Hughes fully acknowledged the influence of these and others upon him. But they would have been the first to have said that the boy with such powers of self-discipline, with such zest for intellectual life, with such breadth of horizon in interest and activity, and with such faith in the enjoyment and utility of memory contributed more to the University than he took away from it. That was indeed the case even while he was an undergraduate. It was yet more notable throughout his long career. As the great reform investigator of the insurance companies, as Governor of New York, as Justice of the Supreme Court, as Secretary of State, and finally as Chief Justice, he reflected credit upon this University. The dividends through 70 years upon Brown's investment of buildings and endowments and teachers in his development repaid the University a thousandfold.

As a student Hughes was not a subject, he was a predicate. He was not inert material upon which the faculty labored; in word and act he was the affirmation of the real college. As an undergraduate he was human, joyous, natural, never stilted or self-conscious, but deeply intellectual, broadly cultural in his interests. Through college and in after years he gained by the accretions of memory and by the development of his reasoning powers an intellectual stature so towering that no statesman with whom he came in contact could surpass him. And his whole personality was strengthened by tough moral fiber. He could not speak an equivocal word; no one could doubt that he meant what he said and said what he meant. During the long period of public service his moral character was in all respects, public and private, without "variableness, neither shadow of turning."

Not everything Hughes did was successful, and he met with stubborn opposition. He was a man as sensitive as any you could find. At least two presidents of the United States did their best to make him miserable, but no one could tell it from his appearance or actions. In the great battle over the Supreme Court, he not only maintained silence but carried his burden with stoic calm—at disastrous cost to his health.

He met with disappointments, for he went to bed in November of 1916 with his election to the presidency announced by most leading dailies and woke up in the morning to find that a handful of votes in California had lost him that great office. Within a year of his death he talked the whole episode over with me in the calm of retrospection. Everything he said showed that he had kept the experience in right perspective from the day it happened, for as long as he lived. He met that stunning disappointment not only with good temper but with generosity; for he lent strong support to the man who had defeated him.

Some of the things he did most successfully turned to ashes. The Washington Conference was as brilliant a maneuver as can be found in modern diplomatic history; yet it did not ultimately prevent war with Japan or lead to the lasting peace for which he labored. But I never heard him express a word of regret for the effort he had made. He had done his best and was willing to take the verdict of history upon that effort.

His life was shadowed with sorrow when illness and death invaded his family. Those who knew him best realized how much family meant, how strong were the ties.

But the observer saw more of gratitude for lives he had shared than repining at their loss.

Charles Evans Hughes was a man among men, who could tell a story with the gusto and liveliness of a great actor, but his public behavior showed a dignity befitting public responsibility. He had as warm and attractive a personality as ever held itself in leash in the discharge of public duties.

He was innately modest. After he retired I urged him, as did many another, to write his memoirs. His answer was always that memoirs tend to employ hindsight to put the best face on the author's own efforts and discount the achievements of his opponents. It was better, he felt, to leave judgment to the impartial historian and the verdict to time.

Whatever place is accorded to Hughes in history, the roots of his greatness were nurtured on this campus in college days. If today this University has a group of students with like self-discipline and similar intellectual drive, with equal breadth of taste and interest, with comparable zest for life, its fame will run the country over and its future will be ensured. And if you learn self-discipline, the rich use of leisure, and the delights of a trained mind, you will take from this Hill a real education.

XIII ☞ Sword of Damocles

T HERE is no major problem in the world today that is not old in substance, even if it appears to be new in form. The problem of hunger is as old as mankind. The problem of poverty has beset the kingdoms of this earth from the earliest recorded history. Ignorance and superstition have for ages held people to fatal courses. Pride, arrogance, greed are deadly sins whose record is inscribed in the first writings that have come down to us. The atomic bomb appears to be new, but it is only a new manifestation of an age old problem—how to balance offensive might with defensive power. Even in its modern form the problem is at least as old as gunpowder. It will do you no good to be deceived by the new envelopes in which old problems are hid.

If, therefore, any of you have come to Brown seeking ready-made answers to the riddles of the world, you have come to the wrong place. I know no better place, but no educational institution has all the answers—nor has any other institution. If any of you have come here thinking that the most important thing is to learn how to make a living, you have most assuredly come to the wrong place. If anyone thinks that by becoming the world's greatest

Excerpt. Opening Convocation, Brown University, September 15, 1952

expert in any field he is certain to make a positive contribution to the welfare of mankind, he is guilty of folly; for the undreamed-of power he might unleash could be used for evil purposes as easily as for the programs that are benign. The expansion of power unmatched by growth in mind and self-discipline merely gives the forces of evil more tools with which to work.

There can be only one justification for the existence of this center of learning or for your resort to it. Here you may make the acquaintance of ideas. If I were to name a single characteristic which is essential to the life—not to say the greatness—of a university, it would be hospitality toward ideas.

A university is first of all a treasure-house of ideas that are old. They have been tested and tried times without number and have not been found wanting. The relationship of freedom to the innate dignity of man is such a one. If you fail here to gain an acquaintance with these seasoned veterans in the age-long war against folly, you will never master the art of learning.

The university is hospitable also to ideas neither old and seasoned nor new and untried; they are still in the process of being examined and reviewed; their temper has not finally been determined, their value is still unsure. Most hypotheses in science are in this group. It is part of the task of a university continuously to subject them to that penetrating analysis by which alone they may come to be rejected as unworthy or finally accepted as a valid part of the world's intellectual store.

Here also, though not often, you may meet with an idea which is genuinely new. That occurs when, with a flash of insight which can truly be called a miracle, some mind seizes upon an aspect of reality and gives it form and expression so that others may recognize and profit by it. A new idea is one of the rare experiences that come to those who discipline their minds, alert their senses, and seek with all their hearts for fresh light on the problems of mankind.

If you do not approach your work in a spirit of hospitality to ideas, the university cannot give it to you. Hospitality is a voluntary act; it can never be the result of compulsion.

Long experience has taught me full well that many of you have already closed down the shutters of your minds —and shutters are sometimes their most efficient part— against this challenge. If you keep them closed, experience will ultimately teach you, but too late, that the attempt to take care of your own business and let the rest of the world go by is a futile hope indeed. If you become a scientist, war can turn your studies for the hope of mankind to its destruction. It makes no difference what vocation you seek to follow, or with what skill or excellence, war or other catastrophe can divert or destroy it.

Your real vocation is not that by which you will earn your living; your great vocation is that of citizen. I repeat: the quality of your citizenship far transcends in importance the manner in which you seek to earn your daily bread. How far we have failed to realize this in America is revealed by our voting record. In this premier democracy of the world—well called the last, best hope of mankind—a bare majority of qualified voters bother to cast a ballot. More people grumble over taxes than express their concern by going to the polls to vote.

I suggest that the world can well afford to wait a while for your productive genius to bud and blossom; it stands in desperate need of your citizenship right now. At a university such as this you can gain both the knowledge and the experience which must underlie good citizenship.

XIV ☞ Farewell to the Corporation

THE depth of my attachment to Brown has become more than I can express in words. I have often thought that no student can walk the paths of the College Green for four years—if he has any sensitivity at all—without learning something from the appearance, something from the atmosphere that its buildings breathe, something from the way history looks down upon him. Even if he were not a scholar and even if the teaching were not so sound and informed and brilliant as it is, he would still be left with an impress from which he would never escape.

If this is true of an undergraduate who spends his four years here—four years which are far from the happiest, four years of that terrible adjustment which youth must make from dependence toward responsibility—the feeling would be multiplied many times for one who has crossed the campus for 18 years, conscious always of its beauty, of its charm, of its history, and of its meaning, but also with the sense that he had a responsibility for preserving and enriching its heritage.

I have worked in many places. I have a strong affection for my Alma Mater. I have respect and affection for Law-

Excerpt from extemporaneous remarks. Corporation Dinner, Brown University, November 18, 1955

rence College, which does so much in so many ways, so inconspicuously and yet so well. But Brown University has been the work of my life; it will always be that, whatever comes.

· · · · ·

There is a peculiar mood in America today. It is best summarized in the fact that Walter Lippmann could write two of the worst books a man could write (*U.S. Foreign Policy: Shield of the Republic* and *Essays in the Public Philosophy*) and get good reviews. The theme of the latter, crowning a life of thought and expression, is that democracy is a failure, that we need to return to an aristocratic government and a strong executive, which means a near-dictator, where the common man shall be ruled and relieved of the terrible responsibility that democracy carries. The book is historically unsound, philosophically defeatist, and morally corrupt. It would never have received decent reviews except that they catch a mood.

We are engaged in a cold war. All the hardware a Budget Director can buy will never win the cold war. We must have the hardware, but the first thing we need is to recover the integrity, the inner faith in the democratic philosophy, in the strength of the democratic structure, and in the wisdom inherent in the people. If the Russians win the cold war, it will not be because they have twice as many scientists as we have, or twice as many engineers, or so many disciplined people. It will be because the Russians have a burning, incandescent faith that they are riding the wave of the future.

If you will go back and read the writings in American history, or merely read Walt Whitman, if you prefer, you will see the unconquerable faith of the past that this nation held the key not only to its destiny but also to the world's need. If we recover that faith, we shall win the cold war. Until we recover it, nothing, not even the cleverness of all the diplomats, can wrest the initiative from the Soviets.

All the statistics say there will be so many students that we cannot educate them. All the statistics say there are too few professors, too few classrooms, too little of this and that. Almost no one says we have achieved already in America more than any other nation has dared to dream of. But that is the fact. We have achieved, since I entered college, a revolution in curriculum and instruction, in temper and tone unmatched anywhere else in the world.

As I go about this country, I visit many institutions, for I am an inveterate bus man when it comes to holidays. I am always impressed with one thing. If the governing boards appreciate what they have, the future of higher education in America will be secure. If I could make you see this institution through the lenses through which I see it, its future would indeed be secure.

Brown has a certain type of conservatism. Almost unconsciously, it has gained enough self-confidence so that it has not followed every fad that appeared across the educational scene. The imitativeness of institutions has been the undoing of many. While sometimes we have missed the boat by not seizing imaginatively upon new ideas, we have let a lot of leaky boats go down without being passengers in them.

I have reflected a long time on these things. I say to you: you have something at Brown which is rare and infinitely precious. If the Corporation can be aflame with faith and confidence in the validity of its ideals, the University will go forward. No river will be too broad to cross, too swift to breast. Anything done in the first 191 years of this institution will be dim by comparison.

I have only one other thing to say: no one could lay down these responsibilities without a sense of release. No one could lay them down without a sense of heartbreak that it seemed necessary to do it in the face of the great opportunities and challenges. To leave these friends, associates, and comrades, to break these ties, is almost more than one can bear.

The only thing which makes it possible is the feeling that these responsibilities have been put in the hands of the right man in the right place at the right time. It is no secret that I have a deep, powerful affection for Barney Keeney. But I have something vastly more important—a profound confidence that, with the magnificent group working with him now and in years to come, and with such members of the Corporation as you beside him, he can by his leadership carry Brown University forward to undreamed developments and strengths.

PART III �ↄ *Wartime*

XV ∽ Character in Action

B ROWN offers the opportunity for an education—but we give no warranty, express or implied, that the seeds we plant will bear fruit. Some doubtless will continue to fall by the wayside, some upon stony places, and some among thorns. But we shall supply all the favorable elements we can.

There are four things here which can help you achieve an education. The first is environment, the second is perspective through study of the experience of the race, the third is perspective through theory, and last, but most important of all, is an accent upon values.

Among these four, environment is the most obvious. Here is a place set apart, equipped and endowed, giving visible and tangible evidence of an interest in the life of the mind. The libraries, the laboratories, the classrooms, and the dormitories—each contributes to that total environment. More important than those physical properties is the company of scholars joined together in a common pursuit of truth, in the great search for understanding and wisdom. There are also your fellow students, chosen with care, coming from near and far, from environments of great diversity into a company of great catholicity. In

Excerpt. Opening Convocation, Brown University, September 24, 1941

addition, there are memories of the men who have been here and have gone out equipped in mind and heart for great events in which they have played significant roles. You profit by the Brown University environment, and if you really gain an education, you also enrich that environment.

The perspective that comes from study of human experience is to be found in history and philosophy, in economics and sociology, in the languages and the literatures, and in the sciences which are themselves but cumulations of one phase of human experience. The interpretations of these subjects by different minds are far from uniform. There is no authentic doctrine of experience valid for all men and all times. What seems deeply significant and profoundly influential to one mind brings no challenge whatever to another. Yet all would agree that the more catholic your responses, and the more critical your evaluations, the more the experience of others will contribute to perspective in viewing the problems which will beset you throughout life.

Theory belongs beside experience as a contribution to perspective. For theory is nothing other than an attempt to give a coherent and relatively compact expression to accumulations of evidence. It seeks to bring order out of the chaos of data with which the mind can readily be overwhelmed. Every effort toward synthesis is consciously or unconsciously an attempt to arrive at a working theory and to give it adequate expression. You must guard against the strange, though common, assumption that theory represents unreality. Quite the reverse, it is an attempt to express reality within a formula that can be seized upon and used by the human mind.

The greatest gift of this University, however, is not to

be found in environment, in experience, or in theory, but in its accent upon values. Standards of value can range from the lowest to the highest. At the bottom is that complete negation of signifiance epitomized in the well-known phrases, "Let us eat, drink and be merry for tomorrow we die"; "By mere chance were we born, and hereafter we shall be as though we had never been; because the breath in our nostrils is smoke, and while our heart beateth reason is a spark, which being extinguished, the body shall be turned into ashes, and the spirit shall be dispersed as thin air."

The postulate upon which this University stands is at the opposite extreme. The college would never have been founded, it would never have survived, it would never have grown and prospered without the sense of value epitomized in the motto upon our seal: "In Deo Speramus." It is a measure of value which puts at the head of the list all the intangibles embodied in human dignity; in the phrase of the Psalmist, "Ye are gods, and all of you are children of the Most High." From that central postulate flows the demand for freedom, for justice, for truth.

If such a scale of values is valid, then other things may have to be sacrificed to maintain them. The physical standard of living, the ease and comfort, the pleasures may have to be sacrificed for a time in order that things of more exalted value may be preserved.

Your predecessors of 165 years ago had no wish to leave this environment and give up their studies, their comforts, such fortunes as they had, and even life itself in the War for Independence. But their studies would have been useless if they had not led them to express their mature characters in action which vindicated the values educated men have always held most precious.

Eighty years ago the issues of the Civil War seemed as confused to many as the issues of this war. Horace Greeley would have let the erring brothers go and the Union be destroyed, just as Herbert Hoover would now let Europe burn itself out. Then students of Brown turned from books to guns with the same reluctance as you do today, and only when it seemed necessary to vindicate in action the fundamental values for which the University itself stood.

The weighing of values forms the great significance of the reorientation of national policy now going forward. It is not an intellectual game. It is not even a cold calculation of national self-interest upon a material plane. What we now witness is the essential character of the American people manifesting itself in a determination to vindicate those values which are most precious.

Some of you will not be called to military service. Others will take training and never fight, and be tempted to feel that you indulged in a futile gesture. For still others the moment of conflict may come. But though the nature of the service required of you may vary, the tradition of Brown demands that you vindicate its accent upon values.

You can do so here and now. Many of you come to your studies under a cloud of uncertainty. You should not let that disconcert you. Those are not idle words of advice; they are designed to remind you that throughout life you will face uncertainties. Those you now face are only more dramatic than others. It is a manifestation of maturity of character to face with steadfastness and with courage the hazards which are part of life itself. That is your reasonable service.

XVI ☞ Quit You Like Men

OTHERS will emphasize that you are going out into a sad world. The world, indeed, is being torn to pieces by the guns in the Far East and in Europe. It is being impoverished by the expenditure not only of treasure but also of human energy and of human life for destructive purposes. In the West and in the East there is a clear moral issue—not an issue of white on one side and of black on the other, but one wherein the shades of gray are markedly different. At the moment, both in the Far East and in Europe, the darker shade of gray is in the ascendant and obscures the sunlight of hope and faith.

We are being assured that civilization as we have known it will be with us no more; that whatever our hopes have been, they can no longer follow the same paths hereafter; that the structure of society, the possession of property, the hope of the world have been shattered.

But I would set before you another view of this issue. If the world is being torn up in the strife, at least there is an opportunity to make the world over. You do not have the problem of a static world. You do not have the issue of inertia to confront you.

· · · · ·

I want to emphasize a point I have sought to make con-

Excerpt. Senior Class Day, Brown University, June 14, 1940

tinuously throughout our association. The future of the world is being influenced upon the battlefields of Europe, but it is not being decided there. When France was defeated in 1871, men said, "The strength of France is broken; her territory is severed; the splendid lustre of military fame that has shone for four glorious centuries is quenched. The future offers a piteous prospect."

When Germany was defeated and crushed 20 years ago, men said, "Not only is their military power . . . destroyed but the military spirit . . . crushed. . . . Now . . . their ships have gone; their foreign trade has vanished and they are condemned to half a century of unremitting toil to repay the loss they have caused. . . . The punishment Germany must endure for centuries will be one of the greatest deterrents to the war spirit." But in neither case did the prophets speak accurately.

Today men say that England and France are already defeated, that the shape of things to come begins to emerge, that America discovers at long last that democracy is a luxury which we probably cannot afford in this kind of world. With all the passion that I can summon I say to you that democracy is not a luxury. It is a necessity; it is a reflection of the dignity of the human spirit; it is the finest flower of political theory; it is the fruit of Christian teaching in the ethical field; it responds to something fundamental, something basic, something deep, and something permanent in the human spirit; if it fails it will be through no fault of the ideal, through no fault of the procedure, through no fault of the theory. It will fail, if it must fail, because your wills are feeble.

The shape of things to come lies hidden in the recesses of your mind and hearts. If your wills are stronger than the will of Hitler, then your wills must ultimately prevail.

If your wills are firmer than the will of Mussolini, then freedom will not be a "rotting carcass" which he may boastfully trample. If you have faith in yourselves, then you have faith in democracy which is set to serve you; and whatever the military outcome of the war may be, whatever the peace drafted upon a piece of paper and signed by one group flushed with victory and another humiliated by defeat, that treaty is "only a scrap of paper" and its fate rests upon the determination, the will power of the men who live in the world.

Down beneath the debris of the war, their voices stilled for the moment by the roar of guns and bombs and the whir of airplanes, are millions of people whose sense of the dignity of life has been outraged, whose yearning for a different manner of life from that to which they are at the moment subjected is powerful. If this great democracy and Canada and Australia and New Zealand hold fast to their democratic faith, if they make such sacrifices in the public interest as their fathers made before them, then the hope of those millions will not be defeated. They will win in times of peace what they may have lost in times of war. Freedom and liberty and all the things for which those magnificent words stand will be vindicated in the world.

The last generation made the mistake of thinking that the world could be made safe for democracy upon the battlefield; when the work of carnage was over, they retired and thought the job was done. The dictators are likely to make the same mistake. If you are steadfast in your desire for a life of dignity and freedom, then their momentary military successes will ultimately come to nothing.

At least you cannot say that you go out into a world where there is no great opportunity. You have before you not only the opportunity but the obligation to remake the world. As you leave this campus, one passage epitomizes all that I have sought to say: "Watch ye, stand fast in the faith, quit you like men, be strong."

XVII ✒ Declaration of War

I SHALL begin by quoting as a text a statement employed by the Nazis as the basis for selecting officer material: "The old ideal of equality of abilities and of patriotic duty to fill-unto-death any post in the army cannot be maintained, because it is a false ideal. It does not consider the individuality of a man and his really greatest usefulness to the Nation. . . . When an entire people is drafted, the most various abilities and special aptitudes become available, and each single man must be placed where he can best serve his country." That was written in 1930, but represents the point of view today.

It is an old saying that the devil can quote Scripture. But when the devil quotes Scripture, although he may do it for his own purposes, he is at the same time conceding the beauty, the power, and the validity of the Word. And when the Nazi war machine seizes upon the basic principle of American individualism in order to exploit that principle, then that principle must have within it something fundamentally valid.

There is at this moment a great temptation to meet the physical enemy at our physical gates. That temptation has been at once the tragedy and the defeat thus far of the

Chapel, Brown University, December 9 and 11, 1941

United States. As you think back over the history of the last 20 years, the concept of our boundaries was too much in the foreground. It is a spiritual tragedy that it took the violation of our material frontier—not the frontiers of our ideas, not the frontiers of our hopes, not the frontiers of our faith, but our physical frontier—before we became a united people. However, this quotation is a reminder that we ought to have as much basic faith in our own system as have our enemies.

If I look calm, gentlemen, it is because it is my business and one becomes trained to be an actor. But I know what is going on in your minds these days. You think you have a transition to make, and God knows you have. You have been brought up under the shabbiest of all materialistic ideals, but I have always felt, and I feel profoundly now, that it has soiled only the outside of the cup.

If I should tell you in detail the things that have happened this morning, you would know that there are tides flowing in the minds and hearts of your elders which are just as strong, just as disturbing as those which run through your own. You must not think as you find it dull to pick up a book, "What is the use of studying history when history is being made faster than I can learn it? Or, what is the sense of studying archaeology when they can make ruins faster than we can dig them?" Those same distracting and disillusioning and semi-hysterical ideas are surging through the minds of the professors also: "Why in heaven's name should I teach this stuff? Here I am wading through, saying the same old thing. It is dust and ashes in my mouth, as though the world I knew was not tumbling about my ears."

You must remember that not you alone, but your fathers, your mothers, your elders, your leaders in Washington and everywhere else are fighting back a sense of hysteria. Consequently you must maintain every aspect of normal activity, for therein is the anchor in life. I was gratified this morning that Mr. Washburn had chosen so beautiful a prayer which could take our minds beyond this instant crisis to the things of ultimate importance. I could listen to the anthem and have some sense that these transitory cares and worries would pass.

There is a strong practical sense in the American people, and the faculty have been looking forward. It was before the declaration of war that they asked me to appoint a committee to look at our curriculum and see what might be done. We hope to reorganize within the framework of the liberal arts, maintaining the fabric of this institution, for the fabric is of fundamental importance. We hope to establish courses which will give you the sense that you are moving in the direction to exploit your individuality most effectively. We shall be in as close touch with what is demanded as any college in the country. When anything is known that can be done, it will be known here; our organization is flexible and alert enough to make the most of it.

Now what is the word to give you? It is simply this, that a change in activity may provide a momentary relief from the sense of strain, it may give you the illusion of achieving something, but its after-effects may be profoundly disillusioning. Because if you do something impulsive in order to start doing something, you may find yourself caught in deadly routine where none of your individuality, where none of your personal power, where none of your gifts may count.

Now mark you this—and I say it after long reflection —I would not lift a finger to keep you or any other boy, including my own, out of the military service. I expect and I hope that you will have posts, not only of difficulty, but of danger. And I have a profound faith that if you will patiently get ready, you will meet both those difficulties and those dangers as resourcefully, as courageously, and as successfully as your fathers and your grandfathers before you. But if you go into those posts of difficulty and danger without adequate preparation, you may sacrifice your lives—which are not so much, for probably three million people have been killed in this war already and I suppose another seven million will be killed later (there were ten million killed in the last war and this is a more brutal one and probably will be longer). I say that is not much, but you would do it needlessly and uselessly, and that would be dreadful, for we do not have lives to waste.

Therefore, I am not looking at the interest of the college, so-called, nor am I looking at your immediate interest, whatever that may appear to be, but I am looking at the basic, the fundamental, the enduring interest of you and your country in saying that you will never be faced with a greater crisis than that which you now face. For to sit still and do one's daily work with these shattering events about us is a very hard thing. If you can maintain a calm and an effectiveness under these circumstances, you will maintain a like calm and effectiveness when you come to the post of fire.

I end, therefore, as I began. Take a leaf out of the book of the Nazis. Move quickly but wholly without haste. We are going to need many men, but men carefully chosen. We are going to need men with clear objectives and not confused activity. We are going to need men with strong wills and disciplined skill. And, I beg you, do not underestimate your enemies.

That has already brought us tragic consequences. The disasters which we immediately suffered should call our attention to the fact that we are fighting an enemy who is brave, bold, resourceful, secretive, and reckless of human life, ready to subsist upon a standard of living incredible to our eyes, and willing to take risks with his men which no officer of a Western power would contemplate.

We go into this war united but deceived by consistent harping upon the exhaustion of Japan economically. The Japanese can operate a military airplane with the amount of gasoline you waste hunting for parking space. The Japanese have used the last 20 years to build a line of secret fortifications in the mandated islands about which we have substantially no information; since the end of the Washington Conference agreements they have been building battleships of a number and size which have remained a military secret. I do not mean to say that the economic potential of Japan is comparable to the economic potential of the United States, but I do mean to emphasize that dependence upon our economic potential alone would be madness. This is war. And war is fought not alone with machines and guns and ships, but with men. All those restrictions about using our Army outside this hemisphere are now swept away—American soldiers and sailors will fight around the world.

There is every evidence that this will be a long war and a hard war, but do not underestimate yourselves. For whatever tides are stirring now in your minds and hearts, you have all the qualities, if you will exploit them, which have made this country great. However, you must have, first of all, a deep, a moving, a powerful faith that what you do as an individual is of vital importance, not only to you but to all your fellows and ultimately to all mankind.

XVIII ☞ Sub-Soil of Peace

I T IS one of the good fortunes of mankind that the
actualities do not always accord with descriptions. For
men are prone to extravagant expressions which, if they
represented reality, would defeat all our hopes and
dreams. Characteristic of this tendency to overstatement
is a phrase worn smooth in the 1940 stream of conversation and official utterance. "Total war" has been used so
often and so widely that it is taken for granted and becomes a barrier rather than a guide to understanding the
struggle. In some connotations and with proper technical
reservations the expression is useful. It indicates the profoundly dislocating effect of war. In a world as delicately
intermeshed as ours, social and economic dislocations
spread in ever widening circles.

In several respects, however, the phrase tends to confuse rather than clarify our ideas. In the first place, this
cliché carries an underlying assumption that total war is
a new phenomenon in human history. Earlier experience
is made to seem invalid, and the concept of a fundamental historical discontinuity is promoted. The assumption and the inferences it stimulates are incorrect and
misleading. It is true that mechanized warfare requires

Phi Beta Kappa Dinner, Brown University, March 7, 1942

the labor of many more workmen for every combat soldier than in earlier times. But the difference is relative. It is true, also, that modern care of casualties necessitates an elaboration of organization which did not previously exist. But the engrossment of the energies of a large section of the populace for the civilian support of the fighting man is no new thing under the sun.

In the days of the French Revolution, for example, there was a "people's army," and everyone was expected to perform some function. The decree, read in the Convention on August 23, 1793, ran as follows: "All citizens must discharge their debt to liberty. Some will give their labor, others their wealth, some their counsel, others their strength; all will give it the blood that flows in their veins. Thus all Frenchmen, all sexes, all ages are called . . . to defend liberty." "From this moment until . . . the enemies shall have been driven from the territory of the Republic, all citizens of France are in permanent requisition for the service of the armies. The young men will go forth to battle; the married men will make arms and transport food; the women will make tents, uniforms, and will serve in the hospitals; the children will prepare lint from old linen; the old men will gather in the public places to rouse the courage of the warriors, to excite hatred of kings and preach the unity of the Republic. National houses will be converted into barracks, public squares into factories of arms, and the earth of cellars will be examined to extract the saltpetre from it. Saddle horses will be requisitioned to complete the corps of cavalry; draught horses, other than those employed in agriculture, will be used for artillery and transport. The Committee of Public Safety is . . . authorized to set up all the buildings, factories and workshops which shall be considered necessary for the execution of this work, and to requisition for that object, in the whole extent of the Republic, the craftsmen and workers who can contribute to success." That indicates a degree of totality seldom attained even in modern war.

The altered status of women offers collateral evidence of the totality of earlier wars. Women do not customarily fight at the front, but it is significant that, following one war after another, their field of activity has been enlarged through the successful exercise of so many additional functions during the emergency. If the wars of the past were merely those of kings and professional armies, as is frequently asserted, the status of women would not have been so profoundly affected.

Whenever, in the past, any war was desperate and long continued, like the Thirty Years' War or the Napoleonic Wars, the casualties, the destruction, the economic and social dislocation, and the impairment of health were so tremendous, relative to the means of recuperation, that they might well be said to have involved a disaster as "total" as the present war. The mask of newness is false.

"Total war" is misleading in another of its inferences. The phrase implies that the whole world is involved because of a newly developed interdependence. Again the change is relative rather than fundamental, for the world has long been more interdependent than we are prone to realize. Spices are to us a luxury or a condiment, whereas once they were essential as a substitute for refrigeration. For that reason they exercised a very powerful drive during the period of exploration and conquest. We may remind ourselves that Columbus was searching for the Indies, that the thrust toward the ocean was occasioned by the cutting of ancient caravan routes in the Middle East. The discovery of America was an incident to a profound dislocation of a vital interdependence. That is a familiar and dramatic instance, but we should remember that it is far from unique; interdependence is old, and the more history is studied the older and more powerful its influences are seen to be.

In yet another manner the phrase "total war" is misleading. It is so magnificently inclusive as to give the impression that all aspects of life are dominated by the war. That is an underestimation of mankind. Human nature has both a profundity and a resiliency which that assumption disregards. The mind of man is so various, so rich, and so powerful that it simultaneously takes into account a wide variety of activities, and, except for moments of overwhelming drama, it participates in many parallel and simultaneous activities which may be lost to sight while subconsciously pursued.

The power of recovery, moreover, is so great that the waters of life can close over a long history of tragedy and display soon afterward an unbroken calm. One has but to read the poetry and memoirs of soldiers or become familiar with their humor to see that even in the midst of the shattering sensations of battle itself there is an intellectual and moral and social life upon a wholly different emotional plane, contrasting with and complementing the dreadful experiences of carnage. Indeed, sanity depends upon ability to hold onto the elements of normal life. "Total war," however, tends to conceal the substantial reality that the economic and social and moral tragedy through which we are now passing is not absolute; it tends also to intimate that there is complete absorption in strife.

Yet the realities are quite different from those inferences. With all its brutalities and terrors, there are vital forces, not only within individual human lives but also within national and even international life, which war does not wholly dominate.

If the phrase "total war" were to be taken in its full and literal sense, then the concept of peace would cease to exist. Yet it is the essence of war as a political instrument that it is a brief and violent means to ends quite different. There must be room outside its false totality, therefore, not only for some other idea but, indeed, for the major idea. Otherwise we are forced to adopt the Nazi concept of war as the normal state and peace as only an abnormal interlude.

At a time when it seems as though all the ties which bind men in unity have dissolved, when so much emphasis is put on the forces that divide us, and when nation is pitted against nation as though for complete destruction, it is worth recalling to our minds that there is a sub-soil of peace. Just as below the surface of the earth there are streams of water, rivers and lakes, minerals and metals, precious stones and many other things of great value, which exist no matter how sterile a "scorched-earth" policy may render the fertile surface, so beneath even "total war" there is a sub-soil of peace. Its riches will still be available when men return from political and economic and social madness to reason and sanity.

Cultural life, by definition, must be catholic. It cannot be circumscribed by a narrow nationalism; its objectives cannot be limited to striking power; it cannot be foreshortened to make a heavy impact upon an immediate crisis. It has dimensions not only in time and space but also in feeling which absorb the shocks of temporary, however violent, calamities. Cultural life, in short, supplies a fundamental continuity in the grand strategy of mankind's history. It is deep enough and vivid enough and vital enough to transcend and overcome tragic discontinuities.

Within a vast cultural framework, which includes all mankind, there are languages far more widely available than any lingua franca, and more a bond of unity than Latin was for medieval scholars. The language of beauty, which finds expression in the arts, is as readily accessible to foe as to friend. It requires no translation, it demands no interpreter, it represents something so fundamental and so universal that it defies censorship. Even though men are forbidden to hear the music, even though the picture may not be reproduced, no censor controls the memory, and no dictator can suborn the imagination.

Part of the great tradition is a common treasury of literature. Its appeal is so universal in space and so timeless in chronology, so deeply embedded in the emotions, that it remains a valid human reserve against any current event, however overwhelming. The Bible has been translated, in whole or in part, into more than a thousand languages and dialects. It contains a historical record of the search for a spiritual interpretation of the universe— for a first cause among transient causes, for an explanation of the meaning of life which is neither ephemeral nor distracted. In the record there set down are all the stigmata of total war: annihilation, pestilence, bestiality, overwhelming grief, courage, faith, the triumph of the wrong and the victory of the right; but through the mad pattern of circumstance is an emerging insight into the mind of God. The partial nature of the attainment of the insights intimated there does not alter their availability.

The record is clear that after the moral order seems to have been abandoned, it exhibits powers of recovery far beyond the anticipations of mere statistical prediction. All great literature shares with the Bible this continuing validity which total war may for a moment obscure, but which remains as a genuine sub-soil of peace. So universal is the treasury of letters that the libraries of the world are not dominated by nationalism. They gather in the literary riches of mankind and make them available in war as in peace. The interchange of ideas and the mutual sharing of the treasures of the mind represent so profound a response to human needs that they defy the pretended totality of war.

There is, consequently, an intellectual comradeship which binds men of every nation together. The great fellowship of the universities is the product of eight hundred years of experience. All stem from common origins; great as their differences are, all have the same fundamental organization; the historic continuity remains unbroken; their tradition defies war. The universities are not merely repositories, not merely saviors of what has been precious; they are dynamic forces dedicated to the expansion of knowledge and the enrichment of understanding. The search for truth is so deeply ingrained in their essential being that it cannot be wholly extirpated, even amidst the fury of battle.

On the surface the air is strident with propaganda, with its deceptive clarity and its calculated obscurity. If the truth appears at all, it is partial and designed to produce an effect; the objective is to rouse emotion and lull the yearning for freedom from its active state into passive acquiescence to official ideas. But far beneath the surface there is a different intellectual climate where the search for truth goes on, truth for its own sake. Studies of pure science proceed with no ulterior motive; philosophy pursues its insights by rigorous logic toward clearer statements of fundamental relationships.

The publication of learned periodicals continues even during war, and great efforts are made to send them, if necessary by devious routes, so that they may be exchanged among belligerents. When that is impossible, reserves are built up, so that at the end of the war files may be completed, gaps closed, and the essential intellectual continuity restored.

The Institute for Intellectual Cooperation is merely the formal reflection of the international character of the search for truth. It is by no means the only agency of intellectual fellowship, but it remains a dramatic and tangible symbol of the dynamic quality of that cooperation.

These and hundreds of other activities represent neither self-interest nor group interest nor national interest. They are dedicated to the ideal epitomized by Goethe, but held by men everywhere whose greatness cannot be confined: "Above all nations is humanity." These things are valid for the whole world and are freely given to it. Not everyone will attain to such insights, but there must be the grain of mustard seed, there must be the leaven in the lump. They are supplied by men who seek knowledge and mature it into wisdom, who pursue truth, not only with single-minded devotion, but with flaming zeal.

This universal quality is reflected in the very structure of the university. Its personnel constitutes a miniature international society, composed of men from many lands. American universities have profited, in this respect, by the bigotry of the totalitarians. They have become a refuge for displaced savants, so that today many who are technically "enemy aliens" continue their studies and their teaching here in America as in England, even in the midst of war. In addition, many native professors have enriched their knowledge and their understanding by travel and study abroad. As the medieval university was characterized by the wandering student, so the modern university is characterized by the internationally trained and experienced professor.

Even more profound than the intellectual aspects of the universal tradition of culture are its moral foundations. Just as intellectual unity is exemplified in libraries and in universities, so also religion and the church which gives it mundane expression are the common possessions of mankind. War leads men to attempt to use the church for belligerent purposes; but however much that institution is prostituted and the precepts of religion defied or misapplied, there remains beneath the surface of total war a sense of human fellowship deeper and more abiding than the strife.

This powerful underlying moral impulse finds expression in humanitarian activities. The oath of Hippocrates binds the physician to adopt a regimen for the benefit of his patients and not for their hurt; it has been the watchword of healing for ages. In the grand balance of life it must not be forgotten that healing has outrun hurt. The phrase "total war," with its implication of total destruction, should not conceal from us the deep reality of total humanity. As the arts of destruction are speeded in behalf of war, so also are the arts of healing. One has only to hear the story of the handling of casualties at Coventry to realize that in the race between damage and recovery the victory is not to the swift bomb alone, but to the blood bank, the sulfa drugs, and the thousand and one advances in the art of healing which remain after the last bomb has fallen.

It should be remembered that there is a sub-soil of peace in the international exchange which makes such benefits possible. During the war there is some tendency to keep new aspects of the medical arts secret, but there is a larger tendency to let them flow across the lines of battle. The wounded prisoner is usually given the same medical and surgical advantages as the soldiers of the native land. Once he is no longer effective as a fighting man, his common humanity transcends his enemy status; the profound moral impulse to save human life replaces the political necessity of destroying it. So also the Red Cross carries its ministry of healing, of information and identification, of amelioration and affection right through the barrage. In the midst of brutality which passes comprehension, there is tenderness which surmounts and surpasses it.

The international aspects of humanitarian interest run far beyond our customary awareness. The United States has participated in literally hundreds of conferences and commissions dealing with such subjects as sanitation, habit-forming narcotics, occupational diseases, safety of life at sea, and many other broadly humanitarian topics. Such meetings have a special quality in that they bring not only the governments of different nations but the citizens of different countries into common thought and action on subjects of great social significance. They encourage realization of the solidarity of world-interest because of the interpenetration of social problems.

In addition to cultural, intellectual, moral, and humanitarian interests there is an enormous range of technical subjects which have been and still are a bond among nations. In this connection it must be remembered that the League of Nations continues to exist. Americans are apt to write the League off as a failure because it did not achieve political miracles. But in non-political fields it has many distinguished accomplishments. Secretary of State Hull declared on February 2, 1939, "The League . . . has been responsible for the development of mutual exchange and discussion of ideas and methods to a greater extent and in more fields of humanitarian and scientific endeavor than any other organization in history."

The fact that the Economic, Financial, and Transit Department is now located in America and carrying forward its work is of first importance. It is well to remember, when one thinks of the coming peace, that there exists a body which has been functioning for 20 years with a permanent staff, with comparable statistics drawn from many nations, and with a series of recommendations regarding free and unrestricted trade of great technical competence, as well as large international implications. Its studies have not been built from the narrow point of view of a single nation but represent an integrated world-economy.

The health services of the League have also survived the war. The Epidemiological Intelligence Report, which summarizes the world picture of the prevalence of disease, is still published each week. Even during the war the League work in nutrition has had startling results. The effort to control the use of drugs through the Permanent Central Opium Board and the Drug Supervisory Body of the League is well established. The effect on the regulation of legitimate international trade and on the reduction of drug addiction and illicit traffic has been encouraging.

Not only was a great deal of technical work centered in the League of Nations, but it also provided a flexible and effective mechanism for the conduct of technical conferences and for continuing attention to their recommendations. The League built up a vast network of expert committees covering not only well-known areas of international affairs but many of important, however limited, appeal. For example, the Committee for Statistical Experts developed standard forms which make the statistics of the several nations both more readily available and more readily comparable.

Furthermore, there is an enormous range of international organizations based upon treaties and conventions defining specific areas of activity, staffed with professional persons, and operating as permanent agencies. These organizations gather essential data, serve as centers for the dissemination of information, or actually undertake the administration of matters of international interest within their limited and usually technical fields.

Even though international exchange broke down, the existence of a Bank for International Settlements dedicated to the effort to facilitate international clearances is important. The maintenance of its structure in spite of the present war lays a groundwork which can be exploited when peace comes. This and all the other technical instruments which have come to maturity and have a solid basis of experience and philosophy are sub-soil resources.

The International Labor Organization has supplied the foundation for cooperation both among governments and among private citizens to the end that exploitation may give way to better standards, which not only ameliorate

the lot of those who have been exploited but which relieve the countries with high standards of an unfair and
destructive competition. It has demonstrated that the
improvement of conditions in one area is of benefit to
all. This basic assumption, now buttressed by a sound
body of evidence, must lie at the center of post-war economic reconstruction.

We are accustomed to say that modern technology has
made us neighbors, although it is not true. It has increased
our contacts, but a neighbor is far more than one whom
we see every day and with whom we rub elbows in the
hurried traffic of modern life. A neighbor is one with
whom there is a feeling of harmony and a sense of fellowship. Neighborliness rests upon moral and emotional
assumptions far more than upon mechanical developments; it grows out of common religious, cultural, and
intellectual possessions which supply a bond of understanding and sympathy. Common technology only makes
them more effective.

Wars are won by the nation with the greatest reserves
most wisely utilized—reserves of man power, reserves of
mechanical power, reserves of industrial power, reserves
of raw materials, and reserves of morale. On the surface,
morale appears to be fortitude in the face of adversity,
enthusiasm over victory. It consists in the long pull, however, of deep spiritual and cultural stability, of profound
faith and perspective. When the war is over, these are the
reserves which remain of most vital importance. And it
is in exploiting them that the solid foundations of peace
can be laid. Underneath, the real basis for morale must
ever be a fundamental awareness of the ultimate issues of
life by which the day-to-day events, in themselves and in
short perspective the very pattern of madness and race

suicide, may be made credible, not to say meaningful.

Lincoln reminded us that there are always sincere people on both sides: "Both read the same Bible and pray to the same God, and each invokes His aid against the other." Beneath these prayers for one another's hurt there is a profounder and more permanent sense of universality —"With malice toward none, with charity for all." It is rare in history to find a fighting leader who exemplifies this sub-soil of peace, but it is always present in a nation, even when it is not expressed with official sanction or with such classic clarity.

The mechanisms of peace are no better than the spirit which animates them. If one had the best engine in the world without the competence to operate it, no tasks would be performed; with the best engine and perfect competence, but without the will to employ them, both the mechanism and the competence would be wasted. As one looks over a world at war, he must ask himself where the spirit to operate the mechanisms of peace is to be found. Where else except in those elements now so deeply buried, but which, nonetheless, exist and represent the only temper, the only mood, the only will that can make the peace viable?

XIX ✒ Perfect Peace

L AST February when I was invited to speak I chose a
text. After wavering between two, I selected the one
from Isaiah, and put nothing on paper, intending to reflect
upon it and see where reflection would lead me. This was
the text: "Thou wilt keep him in perfect peace, whose
mind is stayed on thee." Then came the war and it did
not seem to be a very appropriate text in the new circumstances. I considered changing it, but it occurred to me
that Isaiah wrote those words many centuries ago; they
have stood through many a war. Who was I to run away
from an idea which had stood the test of time?

Each time I reflected upon this figure of speech I was
struck with the words, the "mind stayed." It suggests the
rigging of a ship. The spars stand by themselves, but
under stress they need support to steady them and hold
them erect. In normal times it seems needless to have any
support, but in moments of tension it is obviously essential. When the ship stands idle in the harbor, the rigging
goes slack, but when the gale blows the creaking of the
stays tells the story of their strain. It is interesting to think
also that the support which is given to the spar is quite
different in kind. It is not just supplementary, it is not

Convocation, Wesleyan University, November 12, 1939

a more sturdy stick, but something that relative to the spar itself seems tenuous and slender, yet in stress of weather is vital to survival.

Reflecting upon the figure one has to raise the question, why should the mind be stayed on anything. Is the loneliness of the spar a fair illustration? There is much discussion in college circles of the "ivory tower." The mind dwells in an ivory tower, and by your smiles I observe that you think of it in one sense, while I am thinking of it in a different one. It is utterly alone. No other mind can touch it. No psychoanalyst or any of his ilk can more than dimly and distantly approach it, and they cannot know how much of what they see is really there. This lonely grandeur is at once the glory of the mind, and its terror. For in times of stress and sorrow the mind is not only alone, it is desperately lonely. This indicates both the accuracy and the subtlety of the figure. The mind stands alone like a mast, but it must have outside support of a kind different in character and in quality from itself. Most of the time we are unconscious of the stays, but during stress the need is so obvious that it cannot be overlooked.

Of course, some seek to deny the need; they insist upon self-sufficiency. They face the world with arrogance, rather than confidence, for there is a difference between those two words. Arrogance is a counterfeit; it may appear like confidence, but it does not ring true. The self-sufficient reveal all the weaknesses of the self-made: assertive, without being really sure; scornful of that for which they long. It is unnatural, it is unhealthy to take so arrogant a view and often in times of crisis the mind crashes.

But there are other stays. Money is one of the most common. It is written of a certain man who stayed his mind on his wealth, "I will pull down my barns, and build greater; and there will I bestow all my fruits and my goods. And I will say to my soul, 'Soul, thou hast much goods laid up for many years; take thine ease, eat, drink, and be merry.' " But money is not a support for the mind, it is a distraction; and in times of trouble it is not a strength, but a weakness. It is a fair-weather spar. "Thou fool, this night thy soul shall be required of thee: then whose shall those things be, which thou hast provided?" Money is the most unstable and treacherous of all possible stays.

Still others stay their minds on the State. It is an old device and a favorite one today. I remember, when traveling through Italy a few years ago, seeing a poster of Mussolini in his airplane and the slogan said, "Leave the decisions to him." In Germany under Hitler the people are following the leader in a desperate game, and in Russia the party line is the stay for the Communists, and what a stay! In California just now there is the furor over the "ham and eggs" proposition, certainly a specious security. All those who turn to the State admit the need of a stay, and it is obvious that using the State as the stay offers many things—but not peace. It would be possible to paraphrase the words of our text and say, "Thou shalt be kept in a perfect uproar, whose mind is stayed on the State."

But the text indicates that God is our refuge and our strength—"whose mind is stayed on thee." Here also the figure is both intriguing and suggestive. There is nothing sentimental, "he will take care of you"; it does not promise that God will make the decisions, that He will do the work of the mind. The idea is that the mind will be supported, not supplanted. The promise is that in the moments of lonely terror there will be an awareness of something outside oneself and different from oneself which gives steadiness and strength. It means assurance—and there is no better definition of perfect peace.

Peace is one of the oldest aspirations of mankind. The word appears in the Bible among the most frequent. It appears in literature. Dante's great book, *De Monarchia,* which has been called the climax of the Middle Ages, is one of the most beautiful and moving appeals for peace. And yet the idea of peace is misunderstood. It is not the mere absence of fighting. I am aware that yesterday was Armistice Day; there is an element of dramatic tragedy that we should choose that day to commemorate, for it reveals a desperate, and even fatal, confusion of the mind. It confuses the cessation of fighting with peace. The armistice offered only the opportunity for peace. The fact that we misconstrue it for peace accounts for our irrational readiness to pay the cost of war and our subsequent unwillingness to meet the price of peace.

The failure at Versailles was neither the first, nor will it be the last. One can go back to the end of the Thirty Years' War. One can go back to the end of the Napoleonic War, a hundred years before 1914, when Blücher said, "May the fruits reaped by the swords of the army not be destroyed by the pens of the ministers." Napoleon was banished to St. Helena, but his ghost was not laid.

So we today blame the old men at Versailles instead of ourselves for letting the treaty stand. The Kaiser chops wood at Doorn, a kind of comic figure, after strutting across this narrow world, but the Caesarism for which he stood is again dominant. We helped force a league of nations upon the rest of the world; it was our idea and it was our President who insisted upon incorporating the Covenant into the Treaty of Versailles, but we would not join even after Versailles. It was the United States that invented the idea of the World Court and developed it, but we would not participate even after Versailles.

I am not concerned with the rights or the wrongs of any of those plans. I am vitally concerned with the fatal delusion that the absence of fighting means peace, with the failure to recognize that peace exacts its price no less than war. All that is permanently and tragically symbolized in the fact that any of you—all of you—know the day and the hour and the moment when the order to cease fire was to take effect, but no one of you could tell me the day upon which peace was proclaimed.

Nor is peace a status of calm and inaction. The idea of Nirvana is repulsive. It is not only death, it is worse than death; it is death double-distilled. For without danger, without struggle, without adventure, without risk, the word "life" has no meaning at all. If you are going to sail the seas, you cannot escape the storm and, if you have a mind, you can no more escape storm and stress than can the sailor. From struggle and danger there is no escape.

Therefore, you cannot find peace by seeking to take away the occasions of war, because, if you take away the things about which men have fought, you have absolutely nothing left. They have fought over things of vast significance and things that were trivial, over honor and things material. Over the spoken word men have fought to the death; over the fall of the dice men have fought to the death. Over the smile of a woman, over everything and anything that even remotely touches the well-springs of life men have fought. That reveals the fallacy of appeasement as a road to peace; that shows the dishonesty of the argument about the "haves and the have nots" as a way of peace. For men will fight over small grievances as quickly as over great, and appeasement may create an appetite instead of satisfying it. I am not arguing against justice, but if justice and peace were synonymous this would be a different world, since men have fought as readily, as bitterly, as heroically for unjust causes as for just. I may speak sometime on behalf of justice—but not as a road to peace.

Let us turn this around and face it positively. Friction is essential. You could not walk unless you made contact with the earth—without friction; you could not have electricity without friction; a train could not move, a car could not run. You could not swim unless there was a resisting medium. An airplane requires resistance in order to fly. You cannot erect a building without stresses and strains. You cannot have chemistry without reaction. So peace is not the absence of friction, resistance, stress, or strain. It is the art of confining friction, stress, and strain to useful and positive purposes. It is a condition of fluent power, with friction harnessed.

Peace is the state of assurance that the stress and strain are adequately compensated with proper support. So in the midst of struggle and strain you may have peace. That is illustrated by football. You sit on the bleachers and cry, "Fight, fight!" You enjoy seeing the hard tackle, the charging line, the strong block. Sometimes the struggle is so violent that it brings injury. Yet, though there are struggle and pain, when the game is over it is clear, if it is fought under conditions of sportsmanship, that you have been at peace, because the fighting was confined by the rules of the game and the tradition of sportsmanship;

the stresses and strains were adequately compensated.

Only a personal and international system of ethics based upon God as "our refuge and our strength" can possibly bring us peace. That is the meaning of our text, a "mind stayed on thee." Every other stay that might bring peace has been tried. Each has broken down. We cannot trust man's integrity. That is what made the war inevitable. Men did not keep their word and the loss of integrity is what makes the course of the war a gamble.

When you graduate you will go out into a world at the opposite pole from peace. The hope that the ills of mankind will be cured by the cautery of war is vain. We may hope for some surcease of international strife and pray that it not be succeeded by internecine strife, but peace, "the peace . . . which passeth all understanding," can never be collective. Like wisdom it is available only to individuals. If you would find it for yourself, accept the advice of Job, who suffered agony before he achieved its fulfillment. Then he said, "Acquaint now thyself with Him and be at peace."

XX ✎ V-E Day

IF ONE has lived through this moment once before, his point of view is permanently altered. On that dramatic 11th of November, 1918, I found myself as the executive officer of the State Council of Defense in Connecticut, one part of the Governor's office. I held the office together somehow until noontime and then closed it down. Everyone went up town. Such a scene of madness I never saw before and never expect to see again. Everyone was convinced that we had won the greatest victory in history, as indeed we had, for the fiction that victory was never really won is fiction indeed.

Yet that magnificent triumph and that great sense of exhilaration were the prelude to disillusionment and reaction. We took the fruits of victory, scattered them to the four winds, and set out upon that path which was certain to bring us to the tragedy of this war. Now again we have mastered Germany physically. But it is clear, as clear as daylight, that we have not yet mastered Germany either intellectually or spiritually. Until those triumphs are achieved, this victory in arms is but a prelude to the making of the peace.

Because of the stupidity of those leaders of a beaten

Chapel, Brown University, May 8, 1945

people who would not recognize realities, this surrender has come piecemeal. It will be, whether we will it or no, a hard peace—hard because one half the men of military age are dead, many more are maimed, and others, under the new concept of reparations, will be at forced labor in foreign lands. The nature of our victory is such, just by the happenings of military events, that there is no government upon whom we may throw full responsibility. Consequently, if those people go hungry, it will be said that we starved them; if their economy is not reconstructed, it will be said that we enslaved them.

We must recognize, therefore, that the nature of our victory has laid upon us a vast responsibility, infinitely greater than after that earlier victory in 1918, which was as sweeping but simply of a different kind. We must undertake the control not only of the political life of the surrendered nations which is in chaos, but of their intellectual life which is in suspension, and of their economic life which is in collapse. We assume that responsibility in collaboration with allies who do not see problems as we do and whose concepts of life and the future of civilization are different from our own. The circumstances of confusion in Germany and differences in outlook among the allies make the task infinitely harder.

By direction and indirection we must re-educate a great nation to resume its place in the civilized world. But I say to you, as one whose life has been devoted to education, that you cannot educate people whom you hate. Somehow you must form a harmonious emotional bond. It is difficult enough even between the generations, as you must know, and as I have a lifetime of reason to know. To form this harmonious emotional bond between those who have been enemies, whose language is strange, whose institutions are various, whose traditions are hostile, is even more difficult. Jesus did not underestimate the rigor involved in his command that we should love our enemies.

We shall not educate them unless we also re-educate ourselves, for education is not by word alone, not by knowledge alone, but by example. And if ever Germany is to come back into the comity of nations—and forever to banish eighty million people in the heart of a continent is incredible—that reunion will be achieved only if we set an example of self-reliance and self-discipline which first wins their grudging, and finally their ungrudging, respect.

This day comes almost as an anticlimax. I mention that because it is symbolic of one of the problems we have to face. Yesterday, acting on authentic sources, a newspaper man in a dispatch of classic brevity and of flawless clarity told the story of the surrender; for that act of public information not only he, but the whole organization which he represented, were severely punished. The official mind had come between us and that word for which all mankind was longing. Moreover, the President of the United States and the Prime Minister of Great Britain stood by their microphones and waited for another official mind before they might proclaim this day of freedom. Those incidents represent a new high in officialdom, and that is a barrier to the tradition of freedom as we have known it. In the one case I am confident it was a momentary mistake. In the other it was the reflection of a habit of mind which sooner or later must be overcome if democracy is really to triumph, if freedom is really to reign.

These circumstances are significant because the hope of the world for peace rests upon two pivots: one of them in Washington and the other in Moscow. It is not detracting from the heroism of the British people, it is not discounting the power of the British Empire, it is not looking down upon the amazing cohesion of the British Commonwealth when I say that the key to peace is in the fundamental relationship between the United States and Russia.

We enter now upon a problem of the greatest difficulty. We must deal with a nation larger than ourselves in numbers, larger than ourselves in basic resources, filled with the sense, which we had last time, that they have won the war and that we have been auxiliary. We must work with a nation conceived upon ideas and ideals different from our own. And we must deal with that people in a temper which is neither craven nor boastful. We must make up our minds precisely what we want and how we propose to get it, for if we do not know what we want they will know what they want, and if we do not know how to get what we want they have the perfect pattern for getting what they want.

Some day the story of our relationship with Russia during the war will be told. I suspect it will be a dramatic story, a story of tensions concealed under censorship, of patience winning out in the end, of suspicions being allayed and the fabric of the great alliance being finally held together at the conference in Yalta for this dramatic outcome. From this moment onward all those tensions will be in the glare of publicity. Therefore, it will be, perhaps, more difficult in peace to maintain the fabric of that relationship upon a constructive plane than it has been even during the war. But upon our success in moving together with firmness, with good temper, with sanity, and with courage depends the peace of the world.

If you had been in college eight years ago you would have heard me make my first address to the undergraduates, in February of 1937. I told them that war might well come and made statements about Hitler and Mussolini which precipitated a momentary tempest in the Providence teapot. The war came because we lacked a policy, because we were wanting in steadiness, because we were short of confidence in ourselves.

We had a treaty with Germany which prevented its occupation of the Rhineland, but when the President of the United States was reported to have said in a closed session that our eastern boundary was the Rhine, it became the subject of the most amazing uproar in American life. Today, as our troops are in Prague and on the Elbe and in the North, it seems obvious that he underestimated the case.

Victory has come; we should greet it neither with the hysteria of joy that marked that earlier victory nor with the hysteria of suspicion and fear, the harbingers of which you can already read in the newspapers. We must subject ourselves to stern self-discipline, and I suggest to you that the architect of victory, General Eisenhower, is not at this moment going off on a bender. He is heaving that sigh of relief which must come to a sensitive man when the slaughter ends. He knows he must gird up his courage and his faith for the terrible task of ruling Germany.

As for you, turn now your eyes to the west, first far to the west where men are fighting and dying in the war against Japan. Though the slaughter has ended in Europe, it will rise inevitably to a new fury in the Far East.

Then turn your eyes west to San Francisco where,

amid the blare of publicity, men are building not a peace but the scaffolding of a peace. They are fabricating a structure which is utterly meaningless unless we, the people, breathe into it the spirit of life, unless we bring to the tasks of peace the same spirit of devotion and sacrifice which produced victory on the European front.

XXI ✐ Let Us Remember Them

I SPEAK today with one purpose only—to voice a tribute to those alumni of Brown University who laid down their lives in the war. Most of them were young; some of them very young; some had not even completed the work for their baccalaureate degree.

That fact poses the most critical question I know with regard to the validity of a liberal education.

Whenever I think on the subject, one acid test comes to my mind: suppose that on the very morrow of his graduation the student were to lose his life; would his education have been wasted? The answer is as simple and as plain as any answer could be: if education is preparation, it has been lost; but if education is real and significant as an experience, it has not been lost. Of all educational experience only that of a liberal education is dependent upon no exterior circumstances for its validity.

Liberal education is growth; it is life itself. In the death of these men at untimely ages, the world is indeed impoverished, but, because they had the experience of life in this ancient University, they had been enriched and the quality of their service and sacrifice was enlarged and ennobled.

Annual Meeting of the Associated Alumni, Brown University, June 17, 1946

As we remember these alumni with affection and respect, let us think of them in connection with the life of our nation, and determine so to influence the policies of our beloved country that it shall profit by their sacrifice.

Let us remember them also in connection with this University, and resolve that in all its procedures and all its plans and all its activities Brown will supply to their younger brothers and to all their successors that inspiration and instruction which make even a brief life more intense, more real, and more meaningful.

PART IV ✍ *Postwar*

XXII ✒ Peace—A Step at a Time

EVERYBODY wants to ease tensions and assure peace. The problem is what road to take toward those goals. My thesis is that, having failed to arrive at global solutions for the major problems following the war, we should establish as many limited objectives as possible and direct our diplomacy to the achievement of those useful ends, however undramatic they may appear. Before 1914 such a proposal for limited action would have seemed natural; now it requires a real effort to comprehend it.

The century between Waterloo and Sarajevo saw more evidences of progress toward a peaceful world than any period in modern history. It was by no means a quiescent or stagnant era; indeed it was one of the most energetic in human history. Nor was it free from war. On the contrary hardly a year passed without some manifestation of the use of force for international purposes somewhere in the world. Progress toward the goal of peace consisted in the multiplication of devices to keep wars small, to quarantine fighting with a view to preventing its spread.

The idea of limited war for limited objectives gained such headway that it came to seem normal. The first

Revised and abridged version of speech first delivered at the Naval War College, Newport, September 10, 1951

great war of the twentieth century was miscalled World War I because men had forgotten that before the nineteenth century general wars were common; the Napoleonic Wars and earlier struggles had been as extensive as the political world. Our generation did not realize that the failure of these global struggles to produce global peace was one of the prime reasons for the reversal of emphasis during the nineteenth century and for the effort to limit war both in space and in objectives.

World War I represented not only an abandonment of attempts at spatial containment of fighting; it was global in its objectives, also. At the Paris peace conference statesmen sought not only to solve all the territorial, economic, and political issues; they wrote a constitution for a world government to perpetuate their work.

One might suppose that, when peace was not achieved after the employment of these new concepts during the first World War, men would have been persuaded that such grandiose assumptions were incorrect. Yet despite the collapse of the structure of reparations, the failure of the prohibitions of Versailles, and the breakdown of the League of Nations, the basic notions of "total" global war and an integral world peace continued to dominate international life.

The unfulfilled promises of the Atlantic Charter illustrate this global perspective. The United Nations Conference at San Francisco likewise had a world ideal. The notion that the nineteenth century could teach the Atomic Age anything was rejected. Everything was "globalized" —health, welfare, nutrition, culture, economics, finance, and politics. World-embracing institutions were established to unify all problems under one aegis.

A new set of terms has been tailored to fit the new

structure of ideas. They are usually stated as stark absolutes. One such phrase is "total war." The slogan leaves no room for any different or competing idea. Yet even a few moments of serious reflection make it clear that history shows no instance, ancient or modern, of "total" war. In fact, if every thought, word, and deed were completely engrossed in war, there would be no room for even thoughts of peace; thus war could never end; peace could never come.

"Unconditional surrender" was another verbal absolute which misled even those who gave it currency. It is the proper objective of the military to induce the enemy to yield with a minimum of bargaining. Civilian leaders, however, should never employ as a political concept an idea appropriate only to the military; to do so is to lose touch with reality. If a great power is actually rendered politically impotent, the politician faces an impossible task in making peace. When a political vacuum is created, new forces will rush in to fill it. Unconditional surrender simplifies an armistice; it complicates peace-making.

A third absolute also captured the public mind. With advertising fanfare we were given the phrase "One World." But the neglect of racial, religious, cultural, economic, and a thousand other differences, the suppression of all inconvenient characteristics of reality, made the "one-world" dogma a mirage.

As a kind of reaction from one extreme we are likely to lurch toward another. The one-world concept has now been superseded by a two-world dogma. But biaxiality is as false as its predecessor. Because the United States and Russia are the strongest protagonists, there is a tendency in the United States to forget that neither power dominates large sections of the world, and that they influence other sections in varying degrees. The Asian-African Conference at Bandung should have taught us that much.

The biaxial dogma refuses to admit that a nation can be at peace with both parties and not an active participant in the cold war. This is contrary to history. India, for example, stands today in somewhat the position of the United States in 1793. It is young in years of independence, it faces daunting domestic problems—economic, social, political, religious; indeed it is in more parlous condition than the United States 162 years ago. Consequently we should have some realization that a measure of isolation from the intensity of the struggle may be essential to its survival. What is unquestionably true of India applies in greater or lesser degree to other nations.

The habit of thinking in political absolutes culminates in the incapacity to make wise political decisions. Under absolutist principles there is no way to deal with Russia except by total war. That is a simple, direct conclusion and accounts for occasional demands for a so-called "preventive war." Analysis proves such an idea to be self-defeating, for after force has been employed to the ultimate, politics must still supervene. The effort to substitute force for reason can be successful only in a transient sense; ultimately reason must be the principal implement of political action. From this hard fact there is no conceivable escape.

Recently the limits of political action in dealing with Russia have been very narrow. Experience shows the hope that we could now negotiate a general settlement with Russia to be unrealistic. But again we must beware of absolutes. Because we cannot settle all our problems with Russia, it does not follow that we can settle none. That notion is just as dangerous to sound policy-making as its opposite. It has proved possible, even during the cold war, to relieve some tensions. The Russians withdrew their threat to Iran; they were stymied in Greece, they lost control of Jugoslavia; they modified their stand in the face of the Berlin air lift. There has been an extraordinary gesture lately—the peace treaty for Austria.

Merely to state the proposition, "because we cannot do everything, we can do nothing," is to reveal its absurdity. Yet sometimes public opinion, nurtured on false absolutes, borders upon that attitude. In fact, sentiment of that sort may prove so strong as to damn all efforts at negotiation as "appeasement" and doom them to failure at home even should they succeed abroad.

The sound immediate program is to substitute specific efforts to achieve limited goals for the ideal of global settlement. The British Prime Minister, Sir Anthony Eden, has accepted the thesis that limited objectives are valid. With restraint and good temper, but firmness and clarity, he has dedicated himself to the solution of as many problems as possible, leaving to time and better fortune the resolution of others that can be dealt with successfully only as tensions are relieved. There are clear indications that President Eisenhower is not allergic to such a method.

Progress along even so modest a line requires action of two sorts. First, negotiation must be undertaken wherever there is a chance that it may be fruitful. The objective should be to nibble away in order to reduce the size of the problems for which a tolerable solution seems presently unattainable. That process may not produce dramatic headway toward a general settlement, but the useful is often not dramatic. It may be possible to take only a short step toward peace with long intervals before another step can be taken; yet every advance is worth while.

Simultaneously another sort of action is essential. The free world should be strengthened in order to extend the area of negotiation. That involves continuation of "foreign aid"—in our own interest. There is ample historical evidence that negotiation from "situations of strength" is more likely to succeed than dickering from a condition of weakness.

Here we must be aware that tension between the military and the political branches of the government is normal. The military must try to be ready for any eventuality; that requires more preparedness than the political arm of government is usually willing to undertake. One reason for the tendency of the political branch to go more slowly with rearmament than the military desires is the danger that, instead of producing a situation of strength as a basis for effective negotiation, too large an armament program may eventuate in an arms race, the effect of which might be to postpone negotiation until after war had come and been completed.

It is essential to make the potential enemy respectful of our power, but it is unwise so to stimulate fear as to precipitate rash action on his part. That is why it is the inescapable function of political authority to determine how much preparedness is necessary for negotiation from situations of strength, and how much more preparedness would eventuate in so sharp an arms race as to bring on war. No rule of thumb has the least utility in deciding how much is too much. The practical course is to combine strengthened armament with alert seizure of every opportunity for useful negotiation. If more and more irritations are ameliorated by negotiation, the evidence of adequacy in armament becomes cumulative.

It is true that angry discussion over the partition of Korea and over Quemoy and Matsu shows that some Americans feel no confidence whatever in the validity of limited objectives. Nevertheless, there are indications of a tendency to revive some useful nineteenth century concepts. The North Atlantic Treaty Organization, despite its vast sweep, attempts to handle a limited range of problems in a specific area with which the United Nations could not cope effectively. In the same way the mutual defense agreements between the United States, Australia, and New Zealand made a limited approach to a defined objective. Other neighboring nations are members of the recently organized SEATO.

These are evidences of a dawning realization that many of the world's problems are like food: they cannot be taken all at once or in too large amounts. Like the items in a well-balanced diet, it is necessary to take one bite at a time. The simple truth is that there is so much diversity of interest, even among cooperative nations, that the attempt to deal with everything at once is almost certain to break down.

History strongly suggests that limited action is more conducive to peace. Bismarck offers the classic example of a statesman who followed the doctrine of limited objectives. He abhorred "total" war, not on moral grounds, nor for humanitarian reasons, much less upon sentimental bases. To him all-out war was the height of stupidity because it would prevent reaping the fruits of victory. "War," he said, "should be conducted in such a way as to make peace possible." We do not have to admire everything that Bismarck did to be willing to accept one of his ideas which proved sound.

The reality is that in the long run every peace is a negotiated peace. That the treaty must be acceptable to the defeated nation is re-enforced by the nature—and the cost—of modern warfare. After victory is won, the triumphant nation is virtually exhausted. For many other reasons the moment of victory is brief and the settlements made in that moment are brittle unless they are satisfactory, not superficially but fundamentally, to the defeated. For politics is continuous, while war, even a World War, is episodic.

This is evidenced by the fact that nothing is writ larger upon the pages of history than the reversal of alliances. Within the few years since the last war we have seen a reversal of orientation regarding Italy, Japan, Jugoslavia, and Germany—and toward Russia, in the other direction.

What of Russia? Is there no hope of attaining, if not peace, at least a mitigation of the cold war, a tolerable *modus vivendi?* It will be urged that the ideological barrier is insuperable, that the contrast between the democratic West and the totalitarian East is so great that no accommodation is conceivable.

When that is said, we do well to remember that history is long and memory short. For many years Mohammedans and Christians carried on religious wars. Their enmity was so profound and so implacable that no middle ground seemed available. Now Moslems and Christians manage to live beside each other by curbing their religious intolerance. They no longer use force for purposes of proselyting; neither vows the extinction of the other. Indeed, Turkey has demonstrated its capacity for democratic government and is a member of NATO. This is clear enough evidence that an ancient barrier has fallen; coexistence between Moslems and Christians is a modern reality.

Today we tend to regard the Russian state as it now exists under the Bolsheviks as permanent; but it is scarcely more than 35 years old. In the course of those years it has gone through several phases, during some of which it was, for a time, cooperative. It would be as grave a mistake to regard the current phase as ultimate as it would be to say that it is likely to pass in a brief period of time.

Meanwhile we must be patient with the burdens imposed by essential rearmament until the attainment of situations of strength makes our enemy see the wisdom of negotiation upon a broader base than has so far been possible. For the present a policy of limited objectives can ease some tensions and help preserve us from all-out war which time, and a change in Russia or her satellites, may make wholly unnecessary.

XXIII ✑ The Voices of America

EVERYONE has heard of the Voice of America, but the use of the plural changes the entire train of thought. In any democratic nation there will always be at least two voices—the voice of the government and the voice of the opposition. This is so familiar a phenomenon in the free world that it must seem perfectly obvious. It is worthy of emphasis because it is often forgotten that it has always been so; we tend to regard the confusion of tongues as more characteristic of the current scene than of bygone times.

The reason is simple: history emphasizes what was done, and what was said by those who did it. It spends little time on the alternatives which were not acted upon or on the utterances of those who failed to achieve their purposes; the pages devoted to minority opinion—that which did not prevail—are relatively few. Yet when the actions were being considered and determined, contemporaries heard both sides. Not infrequently the side which prevailed did so by a narrow margin; often the opposition was more stridently vocal than those who won. But since history gives short shrift to arguments that failed, there

Conference of Leaders of Institutes of World Affairs, New York, October 27, 1953; printed in the January 1954 issue of Foreign Affairs

is the natural illusion, common to each successive generation, that the current confusion of tongues is new in the land; in the days of our fathers there was no such cacophony of voices.

Every student of government is familiar with *The Federalist* papers, essays by Hamilton, Madison, and Jay, arguing for the adoption of the Constitution. They have been collected, edited, and are constantly studied for the light they throw upon the meaning of the Constitution. Even the Supreme Court has many times referred to them in its interpretation of constitutional meanings.

But who now refers to "The New Roof" of Francis Hopkinson of Pennsylvania? Who remembers that Luther Martin of Maryland called the Constitution a cup of poison offered to the states and said it forged chains for them? Who now reads Elbridge Gerry's "Observations on the New Constitution," Richard Henry Lee's "Observations of the System of Government proposed by the late Convention," James Winthrop's letters of "Agrippa," or Robert Yates' letters of "Sydney"? The papers written by opponents of the Constitution are seldom consulted save by historians with a highly specialized interest. In 1787 and 1788 the voices of opposition, of Patrick Henry and George Mason from Virginia and Governor Clinton from New York, were loud in the land. Opinion was bitterly divided. With failure, their arguments are relegated to obscurity. History attends upon success.

Men everywhere are familiar with the ringing words of Jefferson in the Declaration of Independence: "that all men are created equal, that they are endowed by their Creator with certain unalienable Rights, that among these are Life, Liberty and the pursuit of Happiness." We know those words reflected a deep-felt faith; they were not the slick phrases of propaganda, since on an earlier occasion he had declared, "the God who gave us life, gave us liberty at the same time." It was a life-long theme. In the last letter he ever wrote he translated the majestic rhythm of the Declaration into the homely vernacular of the Virginia country gentleman: "The mass of mankind was not born with saddles on their backs, nor a favored few booted and spurred, ready to ride them legitimately, by the grace of God."

These are the sentiments which history records. But how often is it recalled that it was said of this selfsame Jefferson that he was "the promoter of national disunion, national insignificance, public disorder and discredit," that he was the friend of anarchy, foe of public credit, enemy of the Constitution, incompetent in office, and a plagiarist? The militancy of his "atheism" was taken so seriously that, upon his election to the Presidency, some nervous people hid their Bibles.

We think of George Washington as the Father of his Country, whose prestige and integrity held together the Constitutional Convention, and who, as first President, took pains to establish precedents that have been authoritative ever since. Very few remember that it was a great patriot who wrote to Washington: "As to you, sir, treacherous in private friendship, and a hypocrite in public life, the world will be puzzled to decide whether you are an apostate or an imposter; whether you have abandoned good principles, or whether you never had any."

We remember Lincoln as the savior of the Republic, whose eloquence once moved men as does that of Winston Churchill. The Gettysburg Address and the Second Inaugural are among the great state papers in American history. It was not a Southerner, but a member of his cabinet, who called him a "long armed baboon" and a "great hairy ape." It was a Unionist, not a Confederate, who wrote less than a year before the Gettysburg Address: "He seems to me to be fonder of details than of principles, of tithing the mint, anise, and cummin of patronage . . . than of the weightier matters of empire . . . he is an unutterable calamity to us where he is."

It is not necessary to multiply examples. Men in public life today are not subjected to anything like the personal vilification which once was common. Character assassination is at a low ebb. The current discord among the voices of America is the normal voice of democracy. We hammer out policy in debate which is sometimes calm, sober, and logical, but sometimes strident, emotional, and demagogic.

There is a second kind of discord in the voices of America. Like the first, it is not peculiar to this nation or to our time. Lack of familiarity with the past is the only reason for treating it as a novelty. The authentic voice of leadership always speaks in terms of prophecy. It is not possible to rouse people to action or to make progress toward some great goal of political or social achievement by using dull and stodgy phrases. Often, however, when statesmen speak on behalf of great aims and high ideals, those hopes are treated as descriptions instead of objectives. That makes an obvious tension between word and act—hostile critics are certain to call it a breach.

Again Jefferson serves as an example. When he said that all men are created equal he was himself the possessor of slaves—human chattels. His beautiful home at Monticello had "ranges," partly underground, where they lived in quarters quite different from his own apartments. It was 87 years before the Emancipation Proclamation put an end to slavery. Even yet we have not learned fully to treat all men as equals.

Every eminent leader manifests to a greater or less

degree this tension—this momentary incoherence—between word and deed. Surely it was true of Lincoln whose fundamental policy was enunciated in the Second Inaugural, of which the younger Charles Francis Adams said with justice, "This inaugural strikes me in its grand simplicity and directness as being for all time the historical keynote of this war." Yet, almost at once, his policy of "malice toward none" and "charity for all" was reversed by the "wavers of the bloody shirt" in his own party.

This same tension appeared in our time. Wilson was a voice of hope to Europe; he was greeted as the greatest moral force in the world. But he was unable in his own day to match deed with word.

These and other statesmen succeeded in that they seemed to fail; they were indeed true prophets, for time has vindicated the vital policies they advocated, and largely fulfilled the great promises they made. The incoherence between word and deed was remedied.

That is the nature of leadership—to establish goals, having faith that time will reverse momentary setbacks. But political opponents will surely draw attention to the disparity between word and deed, and deny its transience; they will almost always attribute the gap between prophecy and reality to sordid motives, or incapacity, or some even less worthy quality. To the admirers of the prophet abroad, who do not have the opportunity to see how well or ill his deeds match his words, the voice of opposition seems like the tongue of slander.

These two manifestations of disharmony are characteristic of all free nations. However, when by reason of size, wealth, strategic position, or other spotlighting factor a nation is under world-wide scrutiny, the effect is greatly heightened. Names which in less conspicuous situations would make only local news are blazoned in headlines the world around. Charges and threats which would be lightly regarded in regions where the protagonists are well known seem much more serious where brief press dispatches give false weight to words drawn from longer context. Only conflict is news, and conflict in a nation with world-wide press services is world-wide news.

The United States has found itself, partly as a result of purposeful leadership and partly in consequence of the logic of events, in an almost uniquely conspicuous position. Therefore, everything that happens here gets disproportionate attention; this accentuates inconsistencies and incoherencies which pass with less notice when they occur in many other countries.

The kinds of multiplicity of voices so far noted are common to all free nations; they simply are highlighted in the United States. However, a third source of confusion abroad regarding what is said here arises out of our characteristic institutions. Certainly among the Great Powers, indeed among nearly all members of the United Nations, the form and theory of our government are unique.

It is a government of checks and balances—legislatively, the House and the Senate are checks upon each other; the presidential veto is a check upon both; and the judicial determination of constitutionality checks both the legislative and the executive. The legislative checks the executive, since it can define the powers of many executive officers, and through its hold on the purse can destroy executive functions by a process of fiscal starvation. The legislative also has a check upon the judiciary because, by legislation, it defines jurisdictions. The President has a check upon the judiciary in that he nominates the appointees thereto.

One of the profoundest beliefs of our forefathers was

that as a government approached democracy it must set up barriers to hasty, ill-considered, or arbitrary action lest it degenerate into mobocracy. Therefore, though they established each of the three branches with certain independent powers, duties, and responsibilities, they also established strong checks and balances so that no one branch might become dominant because of its vigor in the face of the lethargy or inertia of the others. In fact, the checks and balances were so neatly contrived that it seemed likely that the machine could not run at all; only when political parties came into being and became the energizing force was it possible to find any focus of responsibility. At best it is a soft focus!

Historically different departments of the government have been dominant at different periods. Certainly the Supreme Court in the days of John Marshall exercised a powerful influence; it has been said that he reshaped the government. In other times the Supreme Court has been a much less vital force. During the years when Henry Clay, Daniel Webster, John C. Calhoun, Thomas Hart Benton were in the Senate their voices were more influential than those of some of the Presidents.

Two decades before the turn of the century the House of Representatives seemed so powerful and the chairmen of committees so dominant that a brilliant young scholar wrote a book called *Congressional Government*. Its thesis was that Congress was "fast becoming the governing body of the nation," "the gist of all policy is decided by legislative, not executive will." "The business of the President . . . is usually not much above routine. Most of the time it is mere administration, mere obedience to directions from the masters of policy, the Standing Committees." The cabinet members "are not in fact the directors of the executive policy"; "all their duties look towards a strict obedience to Congress." He pictured the President relegated to a secondary position; he envisaged the Speaker of the House as the "most powerful functionary"; he and the chairmen of committees were on the way to constituting something like a parliamentary executive. The author was Woodrow Wilson.

When one reads that book today it seems at least as unreal as *Alice in Wonderland*. With no change in the Constitution to account for it, there has been a revolutionary realignment of power in the federal government. The stripping of authority from the Speaker, the revolt against Joseph G. Cannon in 1910, and the emergence of strong Presidents like Woodrow Wilson and Franklin D. Roosevelt, reinforced as they were by the position of wartime Commander-in-Chief, tended to put the legislature in the shade.

Both Wilson and Roosevelt ultimately faced congressional revolts designed to re-establish legislative influence. President Eisenhower has a philosophy of government which makes him want to yield the point without a struggle; he feels that the division of powers is proper, that the Constitution means what it says, and that the President should not seek to be dominant over the legislative branch. But no President is likely to accede to the situation Wilson described.

As between the Senate and the House, circumstances have led to the voices of Senators being heard more often. The office of Speaker has never recovered its prestige; the size of the House has made unlimited debate impossible; it moves under rules so rigid as to amount almost to gag rule; the power of amendment and the scope of parliamentary tactics are closely trammeled. The Senate, on the other hand, still has virtually unlimited debate; its rules allow a maximum of opportunity for vocal pyrotechnics as well as much room for parliamentary maneuver.

The Constitution gave the Senate an important responsibility in foreign affairs and the Senate has never been without full consciousness of its role. By one device or another it has often sought to expand its power in diplomatic matters. The Bricker Amendment is, among other things, one such. Every effort to make its weight felt more in external relations has given occasion for Senators to speak their minds with great freedom and with some color of authority.

Inasmuch as the President is elected for a fixed term, an adverse majority in either house does not affect his tenure of office. Senators, however, are elected for a longer term than the President; their own positions are often not adversely affected by a show of "independence." Furthermore, party discipline is enfeebled by the fact that Senators acquire chairmanships of committees by seniority rather than by reason of talent or political capacity or any other factor save survival in office. Consequently, they can speak their minds on the floor of the Senate, at press conferences, and in speeches in a manner which may run entirely counter to the President's views. What they say might well, in nations with parliamentary government, be regarded as totally irresponsible; indeed it might bring down their own party government and force them to stand for re-election themselves. No such results follow here. With our tradition of the separation of powers, and in the light of our historical developments, Senators are not only wholly within their rights; their tendency to sound off is taken as a normal part of the "enlightenment" of public opinion.

When Senators occupy powerful positions, such as Chairman of the Foreign Relations Committee or of the Judiciary Committee, they have added influence. If such men say sensational things, their voices will be heard not only in the states which they represent, not only in the United States for which they have responsibility, but around the world. This may give the appearance of divided counsels, or instability of policy, or incoherence in political strategy to a degree which is unwarranted by the facts.

Evidence that discordant voices do not mean incoherent acts is to be found in foreign policy. The great historical lines of our foreign policy have stood rather firm for long periods of time. Secretary of State Hull said correctly that policy attained "continuity of basic objectives because it is rooted in the traditions and aspirations of our people." It has not remained completely unchanged, of course, but certainly it has not been lacking in coherence relative to the foreign policies of other nations.

In all the world there are few current foreign policies older than the Monroe Doctrine, or more consistently pursued. The word "consistent" must be understood in the context of relativity, for the status of Latin America has changed and the Monroe Doctrine has changed to meet the new situation. Moreover, different Presidents have shown greater or less energy, more or less courage, keener or duller insights, in applying the principles of the Doctrine to specific cases where it was involved. Nonetheless, the fact remains that the policy has stood for a century and a third.

Since the Rush-Bagot Agreement of 1817, Canada has been regarded as within our defensive perimeter, though sometimes for reasons contrary to those of other times. When President Roosevelt gave assurance in 1938 that "the people of the United States will not stand idly by if the domination of Canadian soil is threatened by any other empire," he was merely making explicit what had been implicit for over a century.

Since the diplomatic revolution of 1898, close association with Britain has been well maintained on the whole. The reason is simple: the interests of the United States are so extensive that we cannot permit any aggressor to dominate the Continent of Europe. In the twentieth century Britain has been the anchor nation in defense of that policy; we had, perforce, to associate ourselves with it.

Since the war the Marshall Plan and all the nexus of activities which have surrounded and followed it—the North Atlantic Treaty Organization, the Mutual Security Agency, and the Foreign Operations Administration—have been among the most consistent and coherent groups of policies in the world. This remains true without reference to party, to personal leadership, or to all the confusion of voices.

Beneath surface manifestations basic policy touching Asia has also been consistent. We long since determined that no aggressive power should dominate that Continent. The classic form of expressing the objective was embodied in two phrases, "the integrity of China" and "the Open Door," one blocking territorial domination, the other checking economic imperialism. For that essential goal we resisted, then fought Japan; for that central purpose we make defeated Japan an ally and continue to recognize the Chinese Nationalists on Formosa; for that we fought in Korea.

It would be folly to claim perfect consistency. The Battle Act, the Magnuson amendment, and other legislative excursions into the realm of foreign policy have been,

like the Asiatic exclusion laws of earlier days, embarrass-
ing and inconvenient. There have been more such episodes than one could wish. Irritating as several have been,
relative to the great issues with which statesmen have been
called to deal, they have been trivial. The main lines of
policy have been clear, firm, consistent—or as clear, firm,
and consistent as politics will allow, here or elsewhere.

It is impossible to get many different people with many
different backgrounds, all having the right to speak, to
talk alike. The vital fact is that when the government has
acted, its acts have been supported. One would be hard
put to find elsewhere fundamental policies pursued with
more persistence and firmness than those mentioned and
others which could be named.

Is this consistency menaced by recent congressional
investigations? The power of the Senate and of the House
to conduct investigations is not novel; it has not been enlarged. Both houses of Congress have long employed the
practice, which 70 years ago was described as a way to
"superintend" administration. It is a principal means of
exercising a check upon the executive and, for that matter,
upon the judiciary, for Congress has the power to im-
peach judges.

In the present 83rd Congress there are currently being
conducted or have been completed during its life no less
than 39 investigations by committees of the Senate, 48 by
committees of the House, and six by joint committees.
They touch all kinds of problems, such as agriculture,
Bureau of Standards, commerce, elections, disasters,
foreign policy, internal security, refugees, alien property,
military and veterans affairs, and many, many more. Only
a few make the headlines, and they are frequently not the
ones of most importance.

This form of inquiry often performs a vital service. The Teapot Dome investigation under the leadership of Senator Thomas J. Walsh of Montana was one of the most striking manifestations of the power of the Senate and was useful in purging our central government of corruption. When this committee's power was challenged, the decision of the Supreme Court sustained the broad right of investigation; it is not likely to be questioned again, though specific acts of investigators may well be. Even so, such committees do not have some of the sweeping powers possessed by Royal Commissions in the United Kingdom.

Sometimes investigations are conducted with dignity and sometimes in a circus atmosphere. The latter is not a recent development; it long antedates radio and television "coverage." Over 20 years ago Mr. J. P. Morgan, then head of the banking firm which bears his father's name, had a midget popped on his knee and a news photograph taken. It was a breach of good taste and an unkind act; it was irrelevant, but nothing could be done about it. "Loaded" questions and gross unfairness to witnesses are old abuses.

Current investigations are not fundamentally different from earlier examples. Nor do they cow public opinion. Despite all the uproar about the "terror" created by congressional investigations, I do not know anyone with something important to say which the American people ought to hear who has been silenced by the investigative procedures; many who have nothing to say pretend that the reason they do not say something significant is because of those pressures.

There is nothing in the Bill of Rights that promises the freedom there guaranteed can always be enjoyed in com-

fort or in a serene atmosphere. In the long history of freedom, discomfort has always accompanied speaking on
controversial matters. There never has been a time when
there were not social sanctions against candor. But if
freedom is to amount to anything, one must be ready to
pay the price of freedom. When a man speaks out he
must be ready to receive, if not to absorb, criticism.

Many of us wish that Congress would have more regard for its dignity and its responsible function and curb
publicity seekers, bullies, exhibitionists, and others of
like kind. They tend to bring the United States into disrepute because the world is not familiar with this aspect
of the tradition and history of the United States. While
the American people are not completely aware of the
details of this history, they long since learned to take these
episodes in stride; they are not confused even when voices
are shrill. We can only hope that as the rest of the world
becomes more familiar with the United States they likewise will draw investigations into right perspective.

Three factors which seem to create confusion in inter-
preting the voices of America have been mentioned. First
is the unhistorical assumption that there was once a
clearer consensus and fewer diverse voices. Second, tension between prophecy and current performance opens
the way for charges of hypocrisy, often—indeed usually—
unwarranted. Third, the separation of powers lets the
President speak as the official voice of the United States,
but permits members of Congress, who have only a party
responsibility which is often more formal than real, to
speak their several minds as they will.

The fourth and final factor that makes it difficult for
our friends around the world to hear the authentic voice
of America among all the competing voices is our pas-

sion or genius, whichever one chooses to call it, for voluntary association. We not only have more telephones in the United States than all the rest of the world combined, we use them more energetically to organize new committees. Therefore, within the United States we have every conceivable type of pressure group. They are by no means mutually exclusive; people belong to several such groups. Many are "joiners" by nature or acquired habit and may be found in the forefront of numerous causes.

"Pressure group" is a descriptive phrase that often carries an undertone or implication of censure; it is a dog with a bad name. It has the same flavor as the word "faction" had to our forefathers. The makers of the Constitution, and more specifically George Washington, did not want political parties; they regarded them as factions, and, for that reason, strongly deprecated their formation. Yet less than eight years of actual operation under the Constitution proved conclusively that there was no means of getting up steam in the governmental boiler without party stoking. Therefore, within Washington's own official family the division of opinion crystallized on the one hand around Hamilton and on the other around Jefferson, and parties were born.

That was evidence enough that the energizing force for action did not lie within the machinery of government; it had to be supplied from outside. What was true when this country was small, when its population was dominantly of one racial stock and its range of occupations severely limited, was bound to be increased to the nth power when those situations were reversed. The nation spanned a continent; Europe and Asia poured many millions of diverse stocks into the United States; the industrial, commercial, and agricultural revolutions made the economic activities and interests of the constituent elements within the population infinitely complex. All these changes made more acute the need for strong energizing forces to drive the machinery of government.

That this country can continue to have only two major parties is due to their character. National parties are essentially federations of local parties without much effective discipline. Neither has ideological tenets which are consistent; many a Northern Republican was closer to the New Deal than many a Southern Democrat. Often tension within one party on some issue is so severe that it cannot be said to have a policy at all. On the so-called civil rights issue the disagreement between some Northern sections of the Democratic Party and some Southern sections is so strong as to produce a stalemate. There are like dead-center areas in the Republican Party. Before anything resembling party policy can be developed on most points, numbers of factions and group interests within the parties must struggle, if not for ascendancy, at least for an influence upon the inevitable compromise. The natural result is weak party discipline.

Another reason for slack party discipline arises from the fact that all legislators, whether in the states or in the federal government, represent constituencies within which they live. Therefore, a man may have a strong political hold upon his constituency without reference to his party regularity. This is heightened by the habit of nominating in primaries; any individual may announce himself as a candidate for office and, if he gets the votes, can defeat the party machine. In many places personal machines are much stronger than the official party apparatus.

Loose party discipline opens the way for cross-party coalitions that dominate specific policies. One of the most striking illustrations is the "silver bloc" in the Senate. The silver industry is not great in size or in economic terms. But it is concentrated in a few states of rather small population, each of which has, nonetheless, two Senators. When that band of Senators stands together without reference to party ties, they can exact a price (literally a price!) for silver that has no relation to economics.

Even within groups regarded as having solidarity, however, there are likely to be countervailing forces. It is not true, for example, that all farmers have the same interests; it is even less true that they have the same point of view with regard to interests which they hold in common. The differences between the Farm Bureau Federation on the one hand and the Farmers Union on the other sometimes seem about as great as between the National Association of Manufacturers and the Congress of Industrial Organizations.

The farmers must have a voice in America, labor must have a voice in America, the churches must have a voice in America. It is only by organizations uniting and speaking as nearly as possible with one voice that they are loud enough to be heard. But the voices of dissent are never still. The Congress of Industrial Organizations and the American Federation of Labor pursue some common policies, as in hostility to the Taft-Hartley Act in its present form, but they also press for separate goals. The churches of America are united behind certain ideas and ideals, but the Catholic and Protestant churches do not unite on all questions. Wherever one turns, whether to groups of national origin like the Poles and the Italians, or to economic groups such as the farmers, mechanics, and longshoremen, or to religious or to any other groups, there are always rival pressure groups.

From one point of view these rival pressure groups in several fields of action seem to add to confusion. From another point of view their net effect is to establish cluster points around which opinion can form. Thus the public may choose, not from any infinite variety of proposals, but among relatively few put forward in an organized and clear-cut fashion.

The different regions, like the different social and economic groups, must each have its own voice. Within the British Commonwealth the points of view of the dominant elements in South Africa, in India, and in Britain on basic racial issues are quite different. Here, all these points of view are represented within a single compact nation. Our friends around the world will have to learn that the voices of Georgia or South Carolina on some race issues and the voices of New England or the Northwest may be quite different. However, short of a fundamental change toward a monolithic and authoritarian government (for which we have no yearning at all), there will long remain these contrary voices differing in their stress and content one from another.

The root of pressure groups is simple. They are essential; in a country so vast and complex any point of view must be expressed with great energy if it is to thrust its way through all the other demands calling for public action and get a share of public attention. As a matter of practical physics we know that even great energy will not push a blunt instrument far through a dense mass. Therefore, nearly all the drives are sharply pointed. It is, of course, undeniable that the amount of energy expended and the sharpness of the point of approach are not an accurate measure of the inner importance or fundamental wisdom of what is promoted.

An extremely important point needs emphasis: not all pressure groups represent selfish interests. It is one of the evidences of the American genius for voluntary association that many aim to promote the public interest. The organization to support the United Nations, of which the late Henry L. Stimson was a leading figure, was a case in point. The recent Committee on the Present Danger was another. The list could be extended indefinitely. Any contemplation of our habits would fully support the observation of a European, nearly a century and a quarter ago: "If an American were condemned to confine himself to his own affairs, he would be robbed of one half of his existence."

The change in the international position of the United States during the first half of the twentieth century has been so dramatic that it is an understatement to call it revolutionary. Through much of our history, it was possible to view our institutions, our habits, our traits of character as interesting curiosities; they did not have any vital impact upon the rest of the world. Now the world situation is so tense and sensitive that a small border incident between two of the newest and smallest nations occupies the worried attention of the Great Powers; the behavior of a group of war prisoners creates an explosive situation which could eventuate in war. Under such circumstances not only the activities of the United States but even its voices attract an attention quite new in the history of the world.

If we have not yet learned to discipline ourselves to speak softly on matters which affect international policy, it is because we have been as lavish with words as with dollars; we have been as little aware of the damage words may do as we are over-hopeful of the services dollars may perform. Nevertheless, the voices of America are authentic voices of democracy. They are the only means available for attaining any consensus in a nation of continental proportions, which reaches from the tropics to beyond the Arctic Circle and which fronts on both the great oceans of the world. There is no other way by which we may come to a common understanding and a common action.

The vigor, not to say the ebullience, of our people have always been notable. Over a hundred years ago de Tocqueville remarked that in private conversation "an American cannot converse—he speaks to you as if he were addressing a meeting." Today when we speak to one another with a view to determining our policy we sometimes sound as though we were addressing the world. As time goes on, world opinion will come to judge us more by what we do than by what we say in the course of doing it; and in turn, as we gain experience in world affairs, we will learn better how to talk with our own countrymen without needlessly disturbing friendly nations.

XXIV ☞ Fire Bell in the Night

EVERY once in a while an event occurs which does not seem in itself to be of great magnitude, but which is a portent of something vastly significant. In 1820, when the admission of Missouri as a state raised the slavery issue, Thomas Jefferson wrote: "Like a fire bell in the night, [it] awakened and filled me with terror." Of the same event, a Representative from Georgia said, "You have kindled a fire that all the waters of the ocean can not put out, which seas of blood can only extinguish." Ten years afterward all the pollsters would have said that Jefferson's alarm and Cobb's prophecy looked ridiculous, but eventually both were amply vindicated. Great crises seldom mature rapidly; those who read aright the signs of the times may well take thought when they perceive "a cloud . . . as small as a man's hand."

Teachers' strikes should be regarded as "a fire bell in the night." From a quantitative point of view they have not been important. Relative to the huge number of students in our schools and the size of the American educational program, the teaching days lost have been insignificant and the knowledge lost unnoticeable.

The teachers' economic situation urgently called for

Chamber of Commerce of the State of New York, New York City, November 4, 1948 redress; public authorities were laggard in recognizing the issue, dilatory and half-hearted in attempts to meet it. A crisis in salaries was the occasion for the strikes, but it by no means supplies a complete explanation. For nothing is more firmly established historically than that the teacher is poorly paid. One has only to come from a family where teaching has been part of its tradition to be acutely aware of how poorly paid teachers have always been. If there is any labor of love which involves contributed services to a high degree, teaching shares the distinction with preaching. That single fact is all the evidence necessary to prove that teachers' salaries were only the occasion and not the cause of the strikes.

There is no possibility of accounting for the strikes without taking into consideration the drift of many intellectuals away from a profound conviction as to the rightness and the validity of the existing social, economic, and political situation. I mention teachers' strikes first because they are dramatic and easily observed and not subject to argument as to their reality.

So far as universities and colleges are concerned, there is criticism of the "Red" doctrines supposedly preached in the classroom. State legislatures launch investigations. Men lash at the symptoms but fail to make adequate diagnosis. Neither "Red" nor "un-American" is a precise term. Each is an omnibus catchword employed to indicate any disharmony between the teacher and his social-economic-political environment. I agree entirely with what General Eisenhower said last night, that the colleges have very few Communists or even Communist sympathizers on their faculties. But it would be folly to deny that there are many teachers who are intensely critical of our present social and economic structures—both of which seem to some of them to be stratifying dangerously. I am not going to minimize the evidence of the discontent on the part of many intellectuals with the present state of American society and economics.

My purpose is neither to praise nor to condemn. I am essaying an analysis, seeking to make clear what caused the emotional tensions now all too obvious. At the end I hope to present some intimations as to how so dangerous a trend may be reversed.

Perhaps the best place to begin is to point out that many or most of the arguments with regard to the American economic system have no direct application to teachers in schools, colleges, and universities. The profit motive, often described as the mainspring of business, and properly so described, is not and should never become the dominant element in their lives. For example, America has many Nobel Prize winners in the sciences; it would be a shallow and ignorant man who gauged their worth by their income. What is true of them applies also to thousands upon thousands who quietly do their work in schools, colleges, and universities. Without their labors neither our society nor our economic system can survive; yet they function to a large extent outside that system of economics.

That may be one reason why industrialists sometimes find it hard to understand professors. It accounts for the scornful comment so often heard: "If professors had enough ability and the competitive spirit they would not be teaching." Nothing could be further from the truth. Those who do not know the academic world at first-hand seldom have any idea how competitive it is. Nor can they appreciate its hazards. Free enterprise is looked upon by businessmen as the epitome of risk-taking, but the research worker, concerned with advancing the frontiers of knowledge, takes, as President Conant has well said, "a tremendous gamble. Only those who have spent many years in this type of work can ever understand how great is the risk and what the emotional consequences of that risk are." Often a man invests several years of his life before he knows or can know whether his research is a success or a failure. I am intimately acquainted with that risk.

Indeed, I can speak of it at first-hand because after I had spent five years on a piece of research, I asked three experts in the field, all at one university, what they thought of it, and they said there was nothing to do in the field. The same men gave me a prize for my work five years later, but I had to invest those ten years of my life before it could be subjected to the critical judgment of my peers as to whether it was a success or failure.

The professor is a risk-taker, but unlike businessmen, he does not profit financially when he succeeds. A professor of physics or psychology often has to pay for the publication of his most original papers; learned books bring no financial rewards. He receives no patent income from the fundamental discoveries which industry is free to exploit for profit.

Being, in this sense, outside the economic order the intellectual does not share its gains directly. Nevertheless, he suffers from its weaknesses. In the great depression teachers' salaries were cut; in many instances reductions were drastic. Very few colleges or universities escaped cuts; some were very serious indeed. Now that inflation is here teachers are not receiving increases comparable to those of workers in industry.

Professors can say with a great deal of objective truth that they share the losses but do not share the gains. When there is hardship they do not escape it; when there is prosperity they still do not escape hardship. If that is true—and I have never heard it disputed—they have less *firsthand* reason for enthusiastic defense of all aspects of our social-economic structure. They are in a position to consider it from a detached point of view; their observations and conclusions are not biased by self-interest.

Moreover, the nature of their work creates an obligation to be critical. They must re-examine all premises as they look for new truths and fresh insights. Angry objectors to intellectual radicalism assert that professors ought to have an over-riding loyalty. I agree heartily. But their deepest loyalty is like that of the poet—it is to an ideal. As Goethe felt that "above all nations is humanity," so, for the true intellectual, above all other loyalties is fidelity to truth.

The public recognizes this to some degree. For example, no one asks whether the scientist is "radical" or "conservative" when he deals with the atom. He must be willing to follow wherever thought and experiment may lead. The history of concepts of the atom during the last 50 years reveals revolutions in thought of the first magnitude. That is what we expect; we ask only whether the scientist is making new discoveries and expanding the boundaries of truth.

Now this obligation applies equally to those who study society, economics, and politics. We must expect—and not fear—new ideas in these fields. In the best sense of the word professors must be radical, ready to deviate from ancient belief when fresh insights, novel analyses, or additional data so dictate.

Scholars have two reasons for objectivity therefore. They are not part of the main stream of economic life, and the nature of their profession requires them to hold in check emotional commitments which might divert thought.

From both these angles of vision they can see that economics and politics are so closely intertwined as to be inseparable. Economic forces are never left without political guidance; every economy is to some extent a "managed" economy. There is no such thing and has never been such a thing as "laissez faire."

The intervention of the government in the economic system to control (or attempt to control) its swing in one direction or another is the rule, not the exception. Before speaking to you, I read through Alexander Hamilton's famous report of 1791, to be certain that I would not in any way misrepresent what he said. If we were to use modern terms in describing his critically important argument, it would be called an essay in favor of "planned economy." Hamilton specifically rejected letting nature take its course; more particularly he denied "that industry, if left to itself, will naturally find its way to the most useful and profitable employment." Indeed, he asserted without reservation "that the interference and aid of . . . governments are indispensable." He proposed the use of public funds as capital through the public debt.

Hamilton's reasoning was based upon the necessity for proper balance between agriculture, manufacture, and commerce in building a great nation. Without reservation he accepted government responsibility to attain that end. He believed it to be the interest of countries to diversify the industrial pursuits of their citizens. He elaborated the arguments for protection. "Protection," need I say, is a government shield from the operation of economic laws. It is designed to affect prices, profits, and products—all by managing economic processes.

Political action to control economic forces has not been

advanced solely by radicals and this is a good time to emphasize that fact. Hamilton is the final answer to any such notion. Both Democrats and Republicans have long promised—and are still promising—to interfere with economic laws when they hurt; they have both promised —and still promise—to mitigate the harshness of nature's processes in the economic sphere.

It would be possible to give endless illustrations of efforts to control our economy, either directly or indirectly. The academician, familiar with this history, knows we are not dealing with absolutes, but with relatives—not "shall government intervene?" but "how much shall it exert its influence?" He is not so much shocked, therefore, by proposals to manage the economy a little more as is the businessman who has never thought much about the past record.

There is another reason why teachers are critical. They observe and analyze the deviations from orthodoxy upon the part of the priesthood of American capitalism. "Faith without works is dead." Often defenders of the faith in "free enterprise" do not show forth in their actions the ardent profession of their lips.

More particularly, the historian observes that it is not government alone which has prevented the normal functioning of the price system; individuals and corporations have gone even further than government. Many years ago it became necessary for government to restrain private manipulators of the price system. It was a rock-ribbed Ohio Republican conservative, John Sherman, who gave his name to the Anti-Trust Act—the cornerstone of many subsequent policies. I am not holding him responsible for the present fogs of uncertainties, but no one today would pretend that there were not vast economic abuses which made that or some other law essential.

And what were those abuses? They were efforts upon the part of small groups to deflect the operations of economic laws for their own profit. Trusts, cartels, trade agreements, rebates, and hundreds of other practices that will come to your own minds constituted a confession of lack of faith in the beneficence of economic normalcy and an attempt to distort the natural functioning of economic laws. That manipulations have been frequent and formidable is transparent to any objective observer.

The academic critic may be pardoned when he is skeptical that all such practices have now been eliminated and that those who profess complete faith in free competition and the "automatic" operation of economic laws will henceforth show by their acts that they fully believe their own words.

Moreover, business and government are not always on opposite sides. The most notable recent instance was the NRA. It was not designed by theorists, but by practical politicians and hard-headed businessmen so little aware of the fundamental presuppositions of free enterprise that they were ready to abandon their birthright for a mess of pottage. Seeking to meet a desperate situation they threw economic orthodoxy and free enterprise to the winds. Looking back upon the codes and what they sought to do, no candid observer could reach a different conclusion. Even though it may be forgotten by the businessmen who participated with such zest, the record of their economic heterodoxy is there for him who runs to read.

It is well known that I do not advocate a "planned economy"; quite the contrary, I have fought against it in every way possible. On grounds ethical, philosophical, and psychological; for reasons social, economic, and political; to the end that we may have a free society with a dynamic economy, I am for the enterprise system, with as little control as will assure order and establish justice. Before we denounce those who do advocate such programs we must recognize that the economy has never operated freely, "automatically," without controls. That being so we are never offered a sharp, clear alternative: "Shall we have controls, or shall we have no controls?" It is always "how much control?"—a relative, not an absolute, matter.

I have mentioned two broad reasons why intellectuals may easily become critical of our social-economic structure. First: they suffer from its failures; they do not profit commensurately from its successes. Second: scientific objectivity requires them to observe the reality that, when the chips are down, many who argue most ardently against a planned economy support it to a greater or less degree; by their acts they deny their affirmations—or modify them more than they realize.

There is a third reason why intellectuals may be drawn into support of a managed economy. Probably the most massive single economic fact in America today is the public debt. Not long ago able expositors proved to their own satisfaction that there could not be a debt of any such size and that if contracted it could not be managed. Today that once incredible debt is a fact; moreover the management of it is inescapably a public act.

I think the management of that debt and the policies ancillary and incidental to its management have been markedly inflationary. But no one—and when I say "no one" I think I am speaking by the book—has any belief that the debt can be left wholly to the operation of economic forces. When the Chairman of the Federal Reserve Board speaks of having an "instrument of monetary management," and the Chairman of J. P. Morgan and Company, discussing the duties of the Treasury and the

Federal Reserve Board, says, "This is no time for rough management of our economy," the fair implications of such phrases need no elaboration.

It is clear that government action will have marked effects. That would suggest to observers whose profits from prosperity are slender and whose losses from adversity are severe that the government should protect the interests of the so-called "middle class" whose status has been deteriorating alarmingly. They have every reason to know that thus far they are the forgotten men in the management of the debt.

There is a fourth reason for the discontent of many intellectuals, which is not economic but social. There was a time when the significance of their function was fully recognized. The famous Northwest Ordinance of 1787 stated that "religion, morality, and knowledge, being necessary to good government and the happiness of mankind, schools and the means of education shall forever be encouraged." Even earlier, in 1764, the Brown University Charter stated it explicitly: "Whereas institutions for liberal education are highly beneficial to society . . . they have therefore justly merited and received the attention and encouragement of every wise and well-regulated state." Washington's Farewell Address contains words to the same effect.

Those phrases embodied a deep public conviction. For a century and a half to be a professor in an institution of learning was to hold a position of great distinction. One evidence of this was the eagerness of many others to be called "professor"—even phrenologists and magicians. Today, on the contrary, men eschew the title. While it is preserved within academic circles, professors do not like to carry the label outside.

An incidental illustration of the low esteem in which the intellectual is held was the characteristic caricature of the New Deal as a tatterdemalian academic in ragged cap and gown. No future historian will be deceived into thinking that the New Deal was a product of professors. It was fabricated by worldly-wise and vote-wise politicians who changed not only their direction but even their basic theories when it seemed politically profitable. The switch from rigid economy to spending as a way to prosperity epitomizes their readiness to reverse the field. Of course many discontented intellectuals put rational facades upon the operative policies of those who really shaped developments. Yet it was the academics who were pilloried for "crack-pot theories."

Lack of respect for the intellectual is reflected in salary payments. When both salaries and public recognition are inadequate, the normal effect is to alienate those who are so treated.

The decline in the social status of the intellectual has occurred at the most irrational as well as the most inopportune time. More than ever before technology and production are utterly dependent upon the theorist. Few studies were ever more "abstract," few more "remote from daily life" than the pioneer work in modern physics. Studies on the disintegration of atoms during the thirties were sensational in a limited circle—but unknown or a joke to the "real" world. No one thinks them funny now. It was the "pure," "useless" research spreading from university to university around the world which supplied the foundation for the use of atomic energy. If, as is so often asserted, we live in an atomic age, that age was born in the universities.

Similarly, if the government debt is the most conspicuous single datum in our economic life, it is also a fact that it is going to be managed by university-trained economists—good or bad, orthodox or heterodox. They will certainly exercise an influence far beyond that of economists in any other time in history.

As fundamental science must precede applied science, as the theorist precedes the practitioner in industry and in government, so also, much more subtly, but just as really, the assumptions which underlie many of our everyday thoughts and actions spring from the intellectual group. The Kinsey Report has been a best-seller for reasons which I do not understand; it would never have been published but for the work of Freud. Many an advertising man who knows little about behaviorist psychology is governed, nevertheless, in his techniques by what the behaviorists taught. People who would resent being regarded as Marxist in any way nonetheless employ many of his ideas. Indeed a good deal of business practice is predicated upon Marxian economic determinism, though free enterprisers would shudder at the source, if they were aware of it.

John Maynard Keynes was a professor with novel ideas about the economic system. Those ideas when popularized and seized by the politicians have in many ways affected the economic policies of states. Long before he was heard of in business circles he had a keen perception of the power of ideas, for he wrote: "The ideas of economists and political philosophers, both when they are right and when they are wrong, are more powerful than is commonly understood. *Indeed the world is ruled by little else.*" Many an opponent of Keynesian economics vouches for *that* truth. One of those opponents wrote on one occasion: "In the short run, it is true, ideas are unimportant

and ineffective, *but in the long run they rule the world."*
The ideas of the man in the street are often the diluted,
popularized thoughts of the intellectuals.

Emerson was profoundly right when he said: "Beware
when the great God lets loose a thinker on this planet.
Then all things are at risk. It is as when a conflagration
has broken out in a great city, and no man knows what is
safe, or where it will end."

This can be illustrated again and again throughout
history. The French Encyclopedists who turned on the
government in the eighteenth century were criticizing the
abuses of absolute monarchy; their warnings were too
long unheeded and a cataclysmic revolt followed. Similarly, the Russian monarchy many years later lost even
the tolerance of the intellectuals and it was destroyed in
the catastrophe of revolution. In our own time there was
a strong intellectual element—which I can summarize
with the names of Bernard Shaw, Harold Laski, Beatrice
and Sidney Webb, and others that will occur to you—in
the leadership of the Labor Party in Britain which dedicated itself to the fundamental alteration of the nation's
social, economic, and political structure. Intellectuals are
often highly sensitized to the dangers that inhere in a
social system; their warnings may be storm signals which
we continue to ignore at our peril.

Even when an idea is wrong, it may have great influence. It is one of the Marxian dogmas that capitalism
means war. That theory runs counter to two dominant
realities in American life that you and I can see—no
other great power was ever so pacifist as the United States
and until recently businessmen were predominantly isola-
tionist, in large sections of the nation they still are. Thus
the Marxist ideology is refuted by easily perceptible facts.

Yet that does not prevent vast areas of the world from accepting the error as gospel; indeed action predicated upon that erroneous belief is bringing us to the very brink of a world cataclysm at this very moment.

Right or wrong, the intellectuals will have tremendous influence. When decisive responsibilities lie in the hands of any group it is not wise to treat them with grave social disrespect. Yet that is precisely what produced teachers' strikes. Though teachers influence our children, society remained callous to the teachers' adverse economic position until startled by drastic and dramatic action. Public apathy arising from unconscious contempt provoked a forceful reaction. The use of power is inappropriate to the intellectual; he should count on reason and persuasion to attain his ends, and I am not condoning the teachers' strikes. But force, however inappropriate, is always the ultimate recourse when everything else fails.

If one looks at the matter with wide open eyes—devoid of preconception and prejudice—it is clear that the striking teachers were treating society as society had treated them. Because society mistreated them, their respect for the political structure declined. The restraints which should have prevented people with such social responsibilities from making war upon society were loosened. On the basis of *power,* they sought—and *gained*—things which had been denied them on the basis of *values.* As in every war, there were faults on both sides—but the basic fault was the gross neglect by the American public which drove the teachers to substitute pressure tactics for reason.

College and university professors have not yet gone so far. They still exhibit the individualism of the thinker. As President Conant has well said, "Of all the activities of man today the one which must remain most starkly individual is research." Ideas are born in individual minds; they never become communal property until their originality has been lost. Until the scholar finds himself in a hopeless situation, he is loath to organize defensively. He prefers to associate with other scholars only for mutual enrichment from the free exchange of thought, for the satisfaction that comes from the interplay of lively and fertile minds.

But there are clear indications that trouble can develop here as in eighteenth century France, nineteenth century Russia, and twentieth century Britain. It is promoted when businessmen scoff at the theorist, saying: "It may be good in theory, but it is no good in practice." I do not know how many times I have had that thrown at me. Nothing is ever right in theory if it is not true and real, but stupidity and archaism in industrial practice often fail to exploit experimental and theoretical advances. Many a basic discovery has remained too long on the shelf for want of enough industrial imagination to see its possibilities.

Incidentally, there is a touch of irony in the often-heard demand that professors should leave their ivory towers, abandon theories, and do something practical for the benefit of society. Do you know where that idea comes from? It is a Communist idea. They have a word for it; they call it social utility. They want no research without social utility. They denounce pure, free research where a man follows curiosity wherever it leads, and trusts to time and technology to find utility in the new truths he discovers. It is odd indeed to find free enterprisers adopting Marxist views of research. It is another instance of insufficient awareness of the fundamental presuppositions of our own system. If you want free enterprise in business, you must accept free enterprise not as a necessary evil, but as an essential virtue, in the intellectual world.

The theorist, the technologist, and the production man are in an indissoluble partnership; each has his place; but the initiation of the productive cycle is with the professor. It is folly to sell his work short. The self-styled "practical" men are often the ones in error; the least alert are frequently the most critical of the theorist.

Such obscurantism and current anti-intellectualism hold down faculty salaries and prevent adequate research funds from being available. And I speak from first-hand experience because I once worked with a great industry and the only problem that was really hard for me to solve was persuading executives to realize that the more fundamental the research, the larger dividends it would pay in the long run. Something must be done to join the professor's over-riding loyalty to the truth with his natural love of his country and its social-political-economic institutions. The suggestion that we should "crack down" on critics, fire the dissenters, or make them so uncomfortable that they remain silent is the worst possible program. Academic freedom is all the professors have left—and however widely their political, social, and economic views may vary, they will unite in defense of that last bulwark of their profession.

The academic is willing to accept a relatively low economic ceiling. I wonder if you know what this is. I do not suppose there are more than 50 professors in America getting as much as $20,000, and the average salary is under $5000. They are willing to accept a low economic ceiling if they have compensatory satisfaction in terms of social response, if they hold positions of responsibility and dignity and honor which their importance to society

justifies. *Among* the necessities is an increase in salary—
and the need is substantial and urgent. Something had
better be done soon before stark necessity forces the professors to follow the teachers into pressure tactics and
substitute power for reason.

There is one final element in this analysis which calls
for comment. That is a changing balance, or one might
properly call it a growing imbalance, between publicly
supported and privately supported education. There was
a time not very long ago when all higher education and
most of what we know as secondary education were privately controlled. Under the egalitarian principles of
American democracy, as the pressure toward the ideal of
educating all American youth increased, it was inevitable
that there should be increasing public support.

Consequently there grew up systems of public and of
private education—partly competitive and partly com-
plementary. Each has made its own great contribution.
There is no reason for hostility or tension between them;
the public interest requires both. But it also requires that
there should be a reasonable balance between them.
Monopoly, public or private, is as bad for education as
for anything else.

That essential balance is not being maintained. Across
the country the number of teachers employed by the public and paid from the public treasury is now vastly larger
than those employed by "private" institutions. At the
lower school levels the disparity is overwhelming, at the
secondary level it is great, and at the university level it is
large and accelerating. Moreover, salaries in private institutions are falling rapidly behind those in public institutions.

This is a fact of profound relevance to our topic. If a

professor derives a living wage from private sources and if his social status is reasonably comfortable, he accommodates himself to the system which gives him those satisfactions. That is why through most of our history there have not been complaints about radical professors. But if a man's income is derived from the public treasury, he is in no position to object to public management. Moreover, if his salary is larger than that received by professors in endowed institutions, he is going to compare private enterprise unfavorably with public management, for he is better off depending upon the public treasury and would suffer from the fluctuations of private enterprise.

If the time ever comes when all the professors in the colleges and universities of the country draw their salaries from state or federal governments, they may become critical of the working conditions, unionize, and strike as the teachers have done. But they are not likely to be opponents of the expansion of governmental activities. Not being dependent on private enterprise, they will have less and less concern for the fate of the enterprise system.

I must emphasize the fact that it is not alone the professor in publicly supported institutions who is now dependent upon public funds for his salary and research support. Most of the larger private institutions are drawing a high percentage of their budgets, indeed predominant shares of the costs of research in the sciences, from contracts with the federal government. In some institutions this figure has risen as high as 50 per cent or more. I saw a statement from one of the leading endowed institutions the other day, and 55 per cent of all of its revenue, including tuition, endowment, and everything else, came from government contracts. In such circumstances many professors even in endowed institutions no longer look to endowment (that is to private enterprise) to supply the tools of their trade and meet the costs of their experiments, or even a substantial part of their salaries. They have become dependent upon federal funds.

And there is something just a little amusing in the fact that many of us are sitting near the front door with our guns cocked to keep Uncle Sam from coming in, when he came in through the kitchen door long since and is now fully established in the back part of the house. This means that while the argument about federal support of education rages, the real subsidy has already begun; so great is the leverage of these government contracts that many privately endowed institutions would find their programs severely crippled if the contracts were withdrawn.

Professors whose livelihood and labor are not supported by private enterprise, who look to federal funds for both, are not going to resist federal "encroachment," either there or elsewhere.

Count Sforza, now again Foreign Secretary in Italy, commented bitterly during the long years of his exile upon the intellectuals who watched freedom destroyed. All those whom he denounced drew their stipends from the state; it had become their only possible source of revenue and they became subservient to the state. And I say to you in all seriousness that those who have an interest in the preservation of the enterprise system will be well advised to see to it that the private institutions are not weakened further and that government does not engulf or even dominate higher education.

This analysis was not designed as a popular approach; it is a serious effort to call attention to something of profound importance to American life. All the evidence indicates that a larger proportion of young people are to be in school for longer periods of time than ever before in the history of the world. That being so, the temper, the attitudes, and the doctrines of teachers are of vast significance. If, as I have indicated, there has been a growing breach between those who teach and our social and economic system, then it had best be understood.

The cure is not to denounce or to harry the faculties; it is to reform the situation which makes the intellectual bear the burdens without sharing the rewards. It is to recognize his strategic, indeed his vital, place in our economy, our society, and our public life and to proceed rationally and with as much light and as little heat as possible to redress the balance, and give to the teacher that which he must have.

XXV ✒ What about the Reds?

I T IS the test of the scholar that his opinions are founded upon fact, that he does not substitute dogma for observation, and that as the substantive situation changes he adapts his thinking to accord with current revisions of data. The man who takes an attitude and sits on it, while the material for thought is altering, fails in an essential duty.

All of us are disturbed by present congressional investigative procedures. There is historical justification for legislative committees serving as a kind of grand jury, taking testimony as to "rumor in the village" raised to national scope. Modern means of communication and exploitation combined with soundly based anxiety over security have brought the investigations into the public eye.

I spoke of "soundly based anxiety." No one can read the report of the Royal Commission of inquiry in Canada in the Gouzenko investigation without gaining an appreciation of both the reality and the subtlety of the Communist menace, and also the difficulty of coping with it. We in the United States are likely to think that the procedures of that inquiry were infinitely superior to those of our Senate and House. Yet with regard to what have come to

Phi Beta Kappa Dinner, Brown University, March 5, 1953

be lumped as civil liberties the Royal Commission exercised vast powers which are not available to the Senate or the House.

It held persons not formally accused of crime incommunicado for considerable periods; it had power to question witnesses and then put them back in the deep freeze, so to speak, to question other witnesses, and then bring the first ones out again to be re-examined in the light of what had been heard from the others. None could be represented by counsel; none could confront their accusers or cross-examine other witnesses. From the standpoint of procedural protection of the rights of the individual, I have not seen any congressional inquisition which matched the Canadian inquiry in rigor, extent, and penetration of examination, re-examination, and cross-examination. While testimony was not taken under the glare of television and over the radio, and was not motivated by a desire for political profit, it was nonetheless published in full so that anyone could read the complete text—as I did.

The striking fact is that, despite all the practical advantages available to the Canadian Commission, it did not succeed in adding a single name to those revealed by Gouzenko. Furthermore, only some of those cited by the Commission could be proved guilty in court, though there was little doubt of wrong-doing on the part of others. This is clear enough evidence of the subtleties of the danger from Communism; and no one can read that record without being equally convinced of the reality of the danger. The Klaus Fuchs case, the Rosenberg case, and every other instance which has come before courts of law have shown both the seriousness of the threat and the difficulty of proof.

This clandestine international conspiracy is a kind of threat to our peace and safety which was totally unknown when the great guarantees of the Bill of Rights were conceived and embodied in our Constitution. We must be appreciative of this change. Some of the same people who have insisted that other constitutional provisions should be stretched to meet "modern conditions" recognize no change in this area. Yet it ought to be clear that protection of honest dissent should not cover foreign controlled conspiracy.

We must face frankly the need for different laws and new procedures to control the new form of conspiracy. The question arises whether those changes have gone too far. I think they have. We should not endanger liberty to suppress treason.

Few people seem to realize that the executive, the legislative, and the judiciary have whittled away many manifestations of basic rights. For example, by enactment of Congress with the signature of the President "guilt by association" has been established as a valid test of guilt applicable to both citizens and aliens.

Furthermore, in 1947, according to John Lord O'Brian, a distinguished legal authority, there was introduced "a type of trial procedure hitherto unknown; that is, the trial of the issue of the loyalty of a citizen upon secret, undisclosed information obtained from unknown persons or secret agents and without granting to the accused person the safeguards ordinarily afforded in the trial of both civil and criminal cases under the Constitution." The whole situation is made more dangerous by "the new doctrine that our government, in certain civil litigations, has inherent rights as a sovereign which give it a superior and preferential position as against the rights of an individual defendant."

Moreover, by an act passed in 1950 there is authority in time of war or national emergency for the Attorney General *by administrative warrant* to arrest and detain persons "as to whom there is reasonable ground to believe that such person *probably will* engage in or *probably will* conspire with others to engage in acts of espionage or sabotage."

In addition, the growth in secrecy in the operation of the government has added to the citizens' peril. With several of these developments many, if not most, of us are out of sympathy, and yet as citizens we have seen them become reality without effective objection, indeed almost without comment. Certainly people in the academic world cannot hope to have legal privileges which are not accorded to other citizens.

So far as infiltration of institutions of higher learning is concerned, the problem is complicated by misunderstanding about "academic freedom." Some people act as though it were part of the Bill of Rights. From one point of view it rests upon the First Amendment but it has no standing in public law. This particular aspect of freedom is not even conterminous in time with the Bill of Rights. Brown's third president, Asa Messer, was eliminated (to use a neutral word) from his office for making prayers in the First Congregational Church—guilt by association with a vengeance—despite his remaining a Baptist which was all the Charter required. Then such interference with freedom was not a unique occurrence in academic circles; it caused no stir in the learned world. The contrast between the reaction to that episode and the uproar over the resignation of President Andrews because of his economic views shows in dramatic fashion what had happened in the 71 years between 1826 and 1897: academic freedom had become a real issue.

Lehrenfreiheit was an import from Germany. It was not indigenous to the English system from which our academic tradition sprang and it certainly was not indigenous to America. It was, moreover, a considerable time in becoming established and is far from universal even today. We know, for example, that denominational institutions of one kind or another do not provide absolute freedom. The "Fundamentalist" Wheaton in Illinois, the Christian Science Principia, several Catholic institutions, and many others fully demonstrate this fact. Moreover, it is basic to American thought and expression that it should be so; as long as an institution defines its policy, the acceptance of an appointment within it constitutes an acceptance of that policy with all the limitations which may be involved. Even the Scopes trial, despite its circus atmosphere, validated the "legality" of absurd limitations upon freedom. Unhappily absurdity and legality have never been utter strangers.

In the light of all this, it seems extraordinary that anyone could think that academic freedom carried any legal protection in the courts or in a legislative inquiry. It ought to be clear that the writ of academic freedom runs only within each institution. It is a traditional (and seldom precisely defined) relationship between teaching and research officers on the one hand and governing boards and administrative officers on the other. It touches the outside world only in so far as the governing boards resist pressure upon them to curtail the extraordinary degree to which they protect the scholar's rights to freedom of speech under the First Amendment.

Academic freedom consists in this—that a scholar shall not suffer the same social penalties in the exercise of his rights under the First Amendment as other professional persons are likely to suffer so far as that objective can be achieved by governing bodies whose powers are defined by public acts. A doctor, for example, who takes unpopular public positions may suffer in his practice and so in his income. We have seen doctors excluded from hospitals even for their professional views in such matters as birth control or the right to survival between a mother and her child. While there has been professional pressure to defend them, they have suffered social inconvenience and often financial loss as a consequence of these episodes. Acts outside their professional field sometimes bring severe social sanctions and financial loss.

Similarly, lawyers may lose clients and consequent revenue because of actions running counter to public prejudice or, in Rhode Island, as a consequence of a recent churchly definition of their duties as officers of the courts. The professor, on the other hand, suffers neither in tenure nor rank nor salary so long as he performs his professorial duties competently and does not commit gross trespass upon morality or run afoul of the criminal law. He may suffer social inconvenience, but he does not incur social penalties or impairment of his living.

Over the years the privileges which go with academic freedom have not been restricted to matters of professional competence, though the protection of professional opinion is the primary objective of the tradition. It is outside the zone of professional competence that most of the sharp issues which concern the public have arisen. Some faculty members have demanded not as scholars but as citizens a greater shield under the First Amendment than is enjoyed by other professional groups. We do no service to the academic world if we do not face with candor the fact that special privileges and immunities have been claimed in these instances; we should remind ourselves that it is vital to the democratic thesis that privileges and immunities can never be divorced from duties and responsibilities.

This was recognized in 1915 in a statement of the American Association of University Professors which said: If the academic profession "should prove itself unwilling to purge its ranks of the incompetent and unworthy, or to prevent the freedom which it claims in the name of science from being used as a shelter for inefficiency, for superficiality or for uncritical and intemperate partisanship, it is certain that the task will be performed by others—by others who lack certain essential qualifications for performing it, and whose action is sure to breed suspicion and recurrent controversies deeply injurious to the internal order and public standing of universities."

It is important to recall when that statement was drafted. Those days had many characteristics in common with the present so far as emotional tensions were concerned. The European war was on; we were involved, but not at war. We had been asked to be neutral in thought and word as well as deed by the President of the United States and we were being subjected to the most intensive propaganda then available. Passions ran high and there were people in this country who put loyalty to a foreign government above loyalty to the United States.

Historically the fact remains incontrovertible that the profession as an organized unit and faculties as corporate bodies have done little to manifest awareness of this positive responsibility. Sometimes, indeed, the extravagant claim is made that nothing should count in a faculty appointment but professional competence—an extraordinary position, since it would preclude any consideration of gross immorality, for example. This claim totally overlooks the fact that American colleges and universities have never divorced themselves, as did the German universities, from concern with the behavior, character, and morals of their students.

The Brown Charter says that "above all, a constant regard [shall] be paid to, and effectual care taken of, the morals of the College"; explicitly or implicitly a similar injunction is embodied in the academic structure of most other American institutions, including those which are state owned and supported. This objective cannot be attained by police action alone; it calls for precept and example in "the daily association of students with older and well bred gentlemen," as Francis Wayland said.

It is true that many departmental chairmen and many advisory committees, not to speak of administrative officers, have taken character and personal behavior into account in making recommendations for appointment, promotion, and tenure. Moreover, the economic and other disadvantages of the academic life have tended to exclude most undesirables from it. The atmosphere of a college is not conducive, at least so far as the faculty is concerned, to much hell-raising. By the vigilance of departmental and other officers, by natural selection, by economic forces and social atmosphere the scholarly fraternity has attained a high level of character, competence, reliability, and respectability. This is attested in a thousand ways which I shall not labor.

Nevertheless, it is now well known, indeed it is beyond question, that many were tempted by the Communistic promises and principles during the depression. The prevailing pessimism of that time with regard to our eco-

nomic institutions which are inseparably tied to our political institutions tended in that direction, as did the predominant economic determinism of that era. Moreover,
as the prosecutor in the Hiss case said, "There were people
who felt that the advance of Nazism and Fascism . . . was
being stemmed or stopped by nobody but the Russians."
There was a period when, from a distance, it seemed as
though Russia provided, in rare degree, equality of opportunity. Did not an obscure Georgian rise to supreme
power? To many it seemed that in Russia privilege was
not rife, racial discrimination was at a minimum. At that
time the truly totalitarian character of the Communist
regime was not so patent as it is today.

Later, during the war, official censorship concealed
from the American people much of the failure of the Russians to cooperate wholeheartedly with their allies. The
heroism at Stalingrad and the natural sentimentalism of
the American people threw a rosy hue over the Russians;
it is said that the Senate of the United States arose and
applauded as one man over the stand at Stalingrad. There
were statements by Winston Churchill which seemed to
reverse his earlier adverse estimates. There were warm
comments by the President of the United States which
did not require a like effort at swallowing earlier pro-
nouncements.

How many scholars made intellectual, emotional, and
spiritual commitments to Communism, or participated in
"front" activities, is a subject of speculation. Some observers and commentators have assumed that there was a
heavy infiltration of such ideas. I can offer only a personal
opinion based on long observation when I say that the
number was trivial in proportion to the whole.

In thus laying a broad groundwork, I have not forgotten my subject, namely congressional investigations. We have seen many abuses of witnesses, exploitation of inferences, and sly innuendoes. We have seen it taken for granted that error in opinion stemmed from disloyalty. This has gone on for a long time and on both sides of the aisle. There were, for example, the antics of Martin Dies when chairman of the Un-American Activities Committee. Then came the now almost forgotten demand that certain colleges and universities turn in lists of all their textbooks. That involved not only a complete misconception of the way in which books are used and how teaching is done, but an extraordinary burden needlessly laid upon those institutions. Resistance to that outrage was so instant and determined that the inquisitors retreated, though their purpose was not altered. We have seen, in short, a whole list of abuses which have made us expect the worst of congressional investigations.

Now, looking not to our fears but to the facts, we may observe some significant things. First, Congressman Velde has said explicitly that he is not going to hold institutions responsible for having at some time employed people who are subsequently found to have been influenced by the Communist line. That takes away one of the principal threats, the threat to institutions. We do not want federal control of institutions of higher education. That control can be just as serious if it is indirect and unaccompanied by appropriations as it would be if direct and tied to funds. That declaration on his part indicates an important modification of purpose; it distinguishes the current investigation from what had been anticipated. As long as he sticks to it, that is an important reform in investigative procedure.

The second fact we should observe is that so far Senator Jenner has not involved innocent people in his investigation. There seems to be a much more careful analysis of the prospective witnesses and an avoidance of bringing in names recklessly without giving people an opportunity to reply. Indeed, it is an established fact that witnesses, consulted in private, have been courteously treated and when they were frank and explicit have not been publicly pilloried. Senator McCarthy has no part in the present inquiries into educational infiltration.

In the third place, very few people need claim immunity from answering as to their loyalty. Most faculty members do not run afoul of the criminal laws of the United States. It is well established practice that when a man does violate the criminal statutes he loses his rights not alone to protection within the academic circle but to membership in it. When he appeals to the Fifth Amendment for protection from self-incrimination before a congressional committee, it is difficult to see how such protection is necessary unless he has awareness of some act of his which violated the statutes. You cannot incriminate yourself if you have done no legal wrong.

The last and most sensitive issue of all concerns the obligations of men to speak. I think that a teacher, whose professional position under the conventions of academic freedom and whose rights under the First Amendment are more nearly protected from social penalty than any other professional man, has an obligation as a citizen to answer questions relating to his fundamental loyalty.

Appeal to the Fifth Amendment should not automatically lead to severance from one's livelihood. There have been many cases where a frightened man took refuge in that course, though nothing he had said or done was wrong in any way. But it does lay upon the person who seeks that refuge a heavy burden of proof why he should not lose his academic status. It lays upon the governing boards of the institutions which have given tenure to such scholars a clear obligation thoroughly to review their qualifications for continued sheltered membership in a university society.

The public should understand the position of the universities. They have been one of the great influences in American life. They have not been perfect and are subject to criticism, but that criticism should be temperate and fair and accurate. They have not been the home of Communism; they have been bulwarks against it for they are the home of freedom which is the antithesis of totalitarianism.

As public institutions they must stand investigation. It is an unchallengeable fact that Congress has a right to conduct such investigations as those of the Velde and Jenner Committees. But it is the obligation of every citizen to see that those investigations are fair, competent, and constructive and not merely efforts to advance personal ambition by reckless means. Only strong public opinion can bring about the desirable reform in congressional procedures.

XXVI ⚘ Education for Democracy

No one who looks abroad in the world can fail to observe that faith in democracy has ebbed during the last 30 years. From the days of that tyranny-shattering slogan, "a world safe for democracy," there has been not merely a marked recession in confidence in democracy as the best solvent for the world's problems; there is an evident doubt about the likelihood of its survival.

I wish it were possible to evoke from the memories of the older ones among you the triumphant tour of Europe by Woodrow Wilson. There seemed then no doubt in any mind that not only was democracy a valid ideal; it was the most powerful political concept in history—one which had been fully and finally vindicated. No one in the ecstasy of that triumph could have believed that Fascism and Nazism would shortly be born and that Communism would spread like wildfire across half the world—and more than half its population.

For those too young to have memories stirred by that great and dramatic episode in the history of democracy, I wish I might have the power, even for a brief moment, to implant in you a sense of the historic faith in the mission and destiny of America. Sometimes it led men in

Commencement Address, Providence College, June 6, 1950

their enthusiasm to such flights of oratory as that of the character who offered this toast at the end of a liquid banquet: "I give you the United States,—bounded on the north by the Aurora Borealis, on the south by the precession of the equinoxes, on the east by the primeval chaos, and on the west by the Day of Judgment." It was bombastic; it should never have been said, for it was tainted with pride. But without condoning its jingoism, we must still recognize the confidence and the conviction it reflected; both the confidence and the conviction have unhappily vanished.

Instead of songs of triumph we hear much more of "democracy on trial." There is much public comment to the effect that we are losing the cold war; we are urged to "defend" democracy. Indeed, so deeply has the lack of confidence penetrated American life that our opponent in the cold war dares taunt us in the world forum. The spirit of success, Molotov asserted, now animates the Communists, while defeatism possesses the United States. He spoke of our "pessimistic lack of confidence in [our] own strength in so far as the prospect of peaceful competition between states and social systems is concerned." No American made a clear, firm, or explicit answer to the sneer. Unless we break this mood of pessimism and recover the confident temper which long animated our history, we will be beaten without a struggle.

My thesis today is that it is impossible to defend democracy unless one adopts the military aphorism that the best defense is offensive action. This is true because democracy is a positive idea; in no sense whatever does it contain any negative quality. Since it represents, as by its very nature it must, an ideal rather than a status, any description of its current position is disheartening. That is characteristic of any of the primary aspirations of mankind. So the alarm about democracy, now so strident, has always existed in the minds of pessimists and perfectionists. Some men were wringing their hands over the end of democracy as early as the days of Thomas Jefferson; doubters have been wringing their hands ever since.

Any time a survey of democracy is made the result is dismal because the practices of democracy are never in accord with its professions; for as practices improve, the ideal leaps yet further ahead. The eyes of democracy must always be fixed forward toward some distant goal. If they are turned introspectively and self-consciously inward, the result is morbidity. Any negative idea, such as defense, therefore, which implies a fixed position, or a static program, or an immutable boundary, is always and must ever be wholly inapplicable to democracy. If ever democracy is put on the defensive for any considerable period of time it is lost; only when it emphasizes its positive aspect, the primacy of freedom, can it justify itself. That gives the cue for the subject which I wish to discuss today. It is the advance toward democracy through education.

We can *educate* for democracy; I make no apologies for putting a heavy emphasis upon the word "educate." For a quarter of a century the public schools have not been talking primarily about "education" for citizenship. A different word has been used—a word with a different meaning, with implications quite different from the word "education." "Training" for citizenship has been the slogan. The difference between "education" and "training" is not only real, it is extremely significant; for the goals of education on the one hand and of training on the other are far apart. Education looks to wisdom as its product, whereas training looks to skill as its outcome.

The basis of the educational process for many centuries lay in confidence that there were disciplines by which the powers of the mind could be developed and matured. In the twentieth century belief in that idea broke down. The monumental evidence that there were educated and cultured people who had undergone the old disciplines was rejected as proof of their efficacy. By a false inference from science, men fell into the error of thinking that if a thing could not be observed by experimental procedures, it did not exist. Thus there arose a marked skepticism as to whether a liberal education could be a reality.

The new science of psychology was struck with the success of experiments in the conditioned reflex, and many educational psychologists entertained a roseate hope that its techniques would have universal validity. Therefore emphasis was put upon skills readily identifiable and easily measured, rather than upon some nebulous thing called wisdom, which few could define and none could measure.

As the objective of schooling, skill has two inescapable weaknesses. First, its acquisition offers no guarantee whatever that it will ever be used; use depends partly upon demand and even more upon individual attitudes and energies, which are no part of the skill. The second conclusive reason why skill is not an adequate objective is that in itself skill carries no direction. It may be used equally for public service or for public detriment. These two weaknesses are demonstrated by the unsatisfactory outcome of the intensive study of civics, economics, and current events in the public schools and in the colleges over the last 20 years.

The Regents of the University of the State of New York made an exhaustive inquiry into the effects of education in

New York. When the prospective capacity for citizenship of the school children had been reviewed, they published a volume on training for citizenship. A distressing conclusion was recorded: students readily gained information about current events and conditions, but as they learned those facts there was a contemporaneous decline in the impulse to use their knowledge in the public interest. Investigators found no evidence of high correlation between the acquisition of data and the attainment of attitudes and ideas appropriate to democratic citizenship.

It was an old lesson relearned—skill without wisdom is at best sterile, and at worst dangerous. One of the great technicians in teaching American Government—city, state, and national—resigned a famous professorship when he found Tammany leaders using what he had taught them for evil ends. He learned at last that skill alone was not education.

Wisdom functions as surely as skill operates haphazardly. For wisdom is no mere trick, like skill; it is human maturity at its best. The basic technique of training, the conditioned response, has now been shown by the psychologists themselves to be applicable only in limited fields; throughout America educators are reawakening to the need for philosophical coherence among disparate skills. This has led to a fresh emphasis upon what is called "general education."

If we are to *educate* for democracy, we must seek out the essentials of wisdom. The first is perspective. Perspective is attained by broadening and lengthening experience far beyond the boundaries, either in time or space, of the life span of a single individual. Experience, therefore, must be gained vicariously. By imaginative processes the experience of people who lived long before our time and of peoples in far countries must be assimilated into our own lives. Those experiences, though alien in time and space, must come to possess the vividness, the completeness, and the reality of our own memories. They must be reflected upon until they are formed by each individual mind into coherent and significant ideas.

If acquaintanceship with human experience is the method and perspective is the objective, it follows inescapably that remoteness in time or space has no adverse effect upon the relevance of knowledge. The thinking of Plato and Aristotle with regard to democracy is as real, as valid, and as informing as ever it was; the mere nearness in time or space does not make the views of later and less significant people more valuable.

The history of tyranny is long; indeed, the history of tyranny is even longer than the history of democracy. Its transient character and the manner in which it has always nurtured the seeds of its own destruction make it desirable for us to be familiar with its record wherever and whenever it has appeared in human history. It will give us more confidence in facing the Kremlin.

Perspective would reveal the absurd fallacy of the current cliché about "living in a new world." The most urgent problem before the world at this moment is the issue of peace or war. Was that not also the most exigent problem at the opening of the second decade of the twentieth century? Was it not also the central issue as the third decade drew to its close? Indeed, if one gives thought to the matter, the problem of peace is as old as man; it is the tragedy of our time that this basic fact has been forgotten. During the last generation it has been insisted that students had been required to study too much about war and peace and not enough about social and economic matters;

too much of geography and history, not enough about current and local issues.

Neglect to set the central problem of our time in the right historical perspective bears fruit in a generation that does not use the lessons of the past for the solution of its imminent and terrifying crisis. Only a generation which had forgotten the experiences of the world could have been ecstatic about "the outlawry of war"; so transient was that illusion that members of the graduating class have scarcely heard of it, and most of the rest of us have forgotten it. No one with perspective would have expected that prohibition upon war would find an easier path to fulfillment than prohibition upon the use of alcohol.

Only a generation which was obstinately ignorant of the long, informative record of confederations and unions and treaties could have felt so much hope from an organization like the League of Nations or the United Nations. The past would have told them that whatever the forms may be, the substance of success lies in a will to peace, in a steadiness of purpose regarding peace which has been conspicuously lacking.

I would not be misunderstood; I was an ardent supporter of the League of Nations as long as even its shadow remained; I heartily believe in the United Nations and think we should make it one of our principal vehicles of policy. That position is founded upon the belief that through constant use it may *grow* into an instrument of value—and of power. The difficulty has been that we looked upon the League of Nations as a finished product, when only the scaffolding was up; we too often have concentrated our energy upon the framework of the Charter of the United Nations instead of upon the dreary, unheroic, day-to-day task of breathing life into its bare bones.

When we ardently press for a Union of Europe, we forget that pressure, which is essentially transient, cannot blot out the history of hundreds of years which shaped the modern pattern of Europe. That pattern will change. I hope progress toward union will accelerate; but it is naive not to realize that time is an element in politics; and time is something man did not create, cannot control—but must understand.

Perspective, I say, is the cure for many things—the antidote for over-excitement about small issues, the check upon grandiose hopes of global solutions. If one's perspective is right, then the perennial crop of panaceas, every new group of Utopians, and many "catastrophic" events fall each into its proper niche among passing phenomena, and not infrequently among the trivial. There is profound wisdom in the early maxim, "This, too, shall pass away."

It is not necessary to take literally the old saying, "The thing that hath been, it is that which shall be, and that which is done, is that which shall be done, and there is no new thing under the sun." Nor need we believe that the pattern of history is "sealed" or that history reveals "laws" of universal validity. Without going so far, it is nonetheless evident that the shock and terror of incidents decline if we recall that the same sort of thing has happened before, and that the world has survived. On the morrow of the 1938 hurricane, we were told that the glory of New England was gone. But today, when so much of the damage has been repaired, and in the springtime with its smiles, we can realize that wind and flood came before—in 1815 and in 1869; yet the splendor and the glory of New England survive.

What is true of our physical world is true of the world of affairs. As the war drew near in 1939 one of our self-conscious "policy makers" recorded in his diary his "feeling of seeing civilization breaking, of seeing it dying before its actual death." Musing upon the arrogance of this banality—the fruit of knowledge foreshortened and without perspective—ought to be helpful in these days of doubt regarding democracy.

Democracy is not some fresh and untried invention; it is a sturdy growth maturing through the centuries. In Britain and America, at least, its roots have struck deep into the soil. In countries where it was set out as an exotic plant, the intense heat of the World War and its aftermath has blighted it or destroyed it. Where democracy was grafted onto an alien stock, the graft, in some cases, has parted and the bough has withered. But those events, unhappy and unfortunate as they are, do not affect its ultimate validity.

It is perfectly clear, however, that perspective has not been a primary objective in the public schools or in many colleges during the last three decades. Emphasis has shifted to knowledge of today, and to skills immediately useful. The social studies have been crowded with data of the current scene; successive editions of textbooks have tumbled from presses to keep up to date.

The material is out of focus. The simple fact is that the distant past is no more dead to youth than the recent past. If an event happened before he was born, it is just as dead as one which occurred a hundred or a thousand years ago. We may remind ourselves that the students in college today know nothing of the first World War except what they are told; to them Caesar is no more dead, either physically or spiritually, than Woodrow Wilson. Good teaching can make one life as real as the other.

There is, however, one vital difference: the competent teacher can indicate the ultimate effect of the policies of

Caesar, but no man can yet fully evaluate the outcome of the policies of Woodrow Wilson. From the teaching standpoint, in the effort to develop perspective as one of the constituent elements of wisdom, events which are long past (the ultimate results of which can be adequately assessed and fairly evaluated) are often much more useful than those more recent happenings, the meanings of which belong in the realm of volatile opinion rather than of established knowledge.

In recent educational emphasis, distance in space has been treated much like distance in time. The "artificial ties" with Europe, against which Washington warned in the Farewell Address, have been replaced by real ties—with steam and motor vessels, airplanes, telephone, and radio. At the very time when those things have linked us more closely with the old world than ever before, it is held that the teaching of foreign languages is unnecessary. There have been two world wars in one generation, in the course of which nearly four million Americans, who still live, have been abroad. Even in peacetime Americans are the most inveterate travelers in history, so that today one of the principal hopes of plugging the "dollar gap" comes from tourism. Yet when there is more contact than ever before with the peoples who speak other tongues, the teaching of their languages is held to be irrelevant.

The time is coming and is not far distant when we shall watch events in Europe first-hand through the eyes of the camera, and television will draw those peoples across the sea into our own living rooms. Even now many millions of Americans are in direct contact with foreign languages by radio, on the regular broadcast band or by direct short-wave reception. Indeed, Americans are the only people who turn on the radio with the bath and turn it out with the cat. Yet the languages of the world, with all their contributions to perspective, have been caricatured as only "traditional" studies and as having no "magic"; they have been treated with ridicule. The capacity to enter directly into the thought of other people is a fundamental element in perspective.

After perspective, the second important constituent of wisdom as a basis for education for democracy is disciplined emotion. Disciplined emotion is a sound response to values. Such an ideal is as far as possible from the ideal of the conditioned reflex.

If we want to develop a warm but controlled emotional response, we should deal with events and issues where prejudices do not intrude, because prejudice makes for uncurbed emotions. If the matter in hand is wholly detached from current interests and daily irritations, then the discipline of emotion is facilitated. If, for example, a student reads Euripides' *Trojan Women,* he can feel the depth of emotion as Hecuba looked upon the burning city she loved.

> *Ah, me! and is it come, the end of all,*
> *The very crest and summit of my days?*
> *I go forth from my land, and all its ways*
> *Are filled with fire! Bear me, O aged feet,*
> *A little nearer: I must gaze, and greet*
> *My poor town ere she fall.*
>   *Farewell, farewell!*
> *O thou whose breath was mighty on the swell*
> *Of orient winds, my Troy! Even thy name*
> *Shall soon be taken from thee. Lo, the flame*
> *Hath thee, and we, thy children pass away*
> *To slavery . . . God! O God of mercy! . . . Nay*
> *Why call I on the Gods? They know, they know*
> *My prayers, and would not hear them long ago.*
> *Quick, to the flames! O, in thine agony,*
> *My Troy, mine own, take me to die with thee!*

You will not find human passion more poignant, you will not find human loyalty more intense than that. It could have been said by some mother watching the City of London in the blitz, by a victim of Stalingrad, by any woman of Hiroshima; but it is not distorted by the other influences that make those recent tragedies so difficult fairly to evaluate.

Things of the past, in other words, are as "discoverable," they are as new to students, as guessing what Stalin is going to do next. The student can approach them upon an intellectual plane; he can make his emotional response, and then test, in the event, the validity of his judgment of the values. Thus in the classics, now so heartily scorned as "remote" and "dead," students may find, in high relief, the whole gamut of human passions, the whole range of human feelings. They show men grappling with the same moral problems the world faces today. There students may find ideas as clear and thoughts as noble as those for which we hunger at the present moment.

It is infinitely significant that we impress upon every coin, down to the last penny, "In God we trust." But you will look in vain for it carved over the door of any public school in the United States. Attention is no longer given to the eternal verities. Indeed, in this "new" world, in this "modern" flux, anything as stable as an eternal verity is regarded as statistically impossible! Why anyone should expect a healthy emotional response to democracy to develop in such an atmosphere is difficult for me to imagine.

Contrast, if you will, the educational reform of Denmark after it had been stripped of its glories and its possessions. Those who sought to reawaken Denmark and set it upon a new course did not attempt it by showing all the weaknesses and shortcomings which had led to defeat; they did not dwell upon the rape of Schleswig-Holstein, they did not linger over the loss of two-fifths of the land, they did not harp upon economic doctrine, and they did not prate of social amelioration. They said nothing about how the people were clothed or fed or whether a third of them had too much or a third of them had too little.

Instead, they carried the peasants back to the folk songs, the old legends, the stories of ancient days—to the wisdom of the ages. They sought to inspire those beaten youth, they sought to reawaken courage and the spirit of piety. Christian Kold exclaimed on one occasion, "When I am inspired I can speak so that my hearers will remember what I say even beyond this world"! Their aim, in other words, was not to bring the facts of everyday life to the youth of beaten Denmark; it was disciplined emotion which they had as their goal. They believed that, if you awaken courage and inculcate a sound judgment of values, then knowledge will take care of itself. If minds are stimulated and hearts are warmed, then the formulation of policy also will take care of itself. The event has proved they were abundantly right.

The process in America has been the precise reverse. Determinedly, the story of the race, on the social and the political side, has been robbed of the sense of victory and achievement; it is all too often interpreted as a record of exploitation and frustration. In fact, the only "success story" currently popular in the public schools is in the field of science, which is ethically neutral, and serves with even hand the will bent upon constructive effort or destructive purpose.

The emphasis has been shifted from the triumphs in American life to its shortcomings and its failures. We hear little now of the rise from the cabin to the presidency; we hear less and less of the gifts of the industrial revolution, which has brought the slaves of the lamp and many other

slaves to do our bidding, and more and more of techno-
logical unemployment, until fear rather than courage is
the emotion which we inspire.

Democracy, itself, has been criticized as not giving "security." If one seeks to discipline emotional response for
life in a democracy, I say to you that security is the worst
possible ideal. When Woodrow Wilson asked for a world
safe for democracy, Gilbert Chesterton retorted, "Impossible; democracy is a dangerous trade." So indeed it is,
for if democracy does not live dangerously, then democracy does not live at all.

If you set up a political slogan of "Safety first," it is
corrosive of the very central ideal of democracy. Democracy requires the pursuit of many ideals and their pursuit
is always inherently hazardous; to set safety above them
ends our pursuit before it is fairly started. It is, therefore,
no accident that an age which has made a fetish of "security," an age which seeks to escape the hazards of life, has
not been effective educationally in forwarding the democratic ideal. Democracy is a great human adventure, and
only the adventurous spirit makes it possible. The sense
of adventure is an emotional matter, and education must
deal constructively with the emotions as well as with the
intellect.

There is a third aspect of wisdom of which I would
speak. Wisdom is not easily acquired. "For at the first she
will walk with him in crooked ways, and will bring fear
and dread upon him, and torment him with her discipline.
. . . If he go astray, she will forsake him, and give him
over to his fall." Patience is necessary, but industry is
even more so. Industry is the third important constituent
of wisdom, yet the virtue of hard work is selling at a
serious discount in the public schools of America.

So meanly do we regard our children that one of the

commonest assertions is that the disciplines which have so long charmed the minds of men are "too hard." Schools doubtful of their own programs, schools crowded with students kept there against their wills by the law of the land, schools under political pressure to "pass" their students, schools suddenly supersensitive to the psychological dangers involved in the concept of failure have tended consistently to substitute less and less arduous and infinitely less significant materials of instruction. It is a self-defeating program, if wisdom is our goal.

It has been preached for 25 years now that the failure of the student is the failure of the teacher, as though failure were not one of the common, one of the inescapable experiences of life. "Passing the buck" for failure from the student to the instructor establishes an escape mechanism that will exact a dreadful toll in years to come. Learning by industry and by foresight to escape failure is one of life's greatest lessons, and to short-circuit that lesson by abolishing failure by edict is to give a false definition of success and to lend an illusion of achievement where none exists. Such a course of action, whatever the motive, must put industry at a discount, just as blaming things on "society" relieves the individual of his sense of personal responsibility.

No one wants to abuse the youth of today, but we are in far more danger of killing them by mistaken kindness than by overwork. Much, of course, can be done by modern devices to facilitate instruction. But when the last movie reel is put back in its tin box and all the sugar-coating has been sucked from the pill, the process of learning will still be difficult. Whoever pretends that it is easy is cheating our youth. Any procedure which miscalls failure by the name of success does not advance, but prevents, education. Any refusal to make a boy face ideas, because ideas are more difficut to grasp than facts, results in simply stuffing him instead of educating him. Any pretense that the material can really be "correlated" outside his own mind misleads him.

Learning, the use of the mind, is hard work. It requires industry of a courageous kind. I have seen many a boy who would sweat all summer building roads quail before a book. But books must be faced; and even worse awaits. What is there must be remembered and reflected upon until it is no longer a piece of a book stuck into the mind, but until the ideas are digested and become an integral part of the mind, just as food well digested becomes part of the body.

Democracy is the most difficult, it is the most dangerous form of government. It achieves progress in the hardest possible way, in the belief that the process is as important as the result. That process is the realization of the fullest potentiality of each individual citizen—not merely his most convenient use by the state, but his richest self-realization. To that end the state, in normal times, waits upon his voluntary activity for the solution of its hardest problems. Democracy seeks to fulfill that ancient ideal: "The multitude of the wise is the welfare of the world." That ideal can never be attained by training for skills alone; it may be attained by education for wisdom— through perspective, response to values, and industry.